# Crafting
## THREAD JEWELRY

THE BEGINNER'S ESSENTIAL GUIDE TO CREATING GORGEOUS THREAD WRAPPED BRACELETS, EARRINGS, NECKLACES, AND PINS INSPIRED BY TRADITIONAL DORSET BUTTONS

PAT OLSKI

YarnWhirled Press

Copyright © 2021 by Pat Olski

Cover design, illustrations, images, and text copyright © 2021 by Pat Olski

All rights reserved. No part of this book may be reproduced in any form or by any electronic or mechanical means, including information storage and retrieval systems, without permission in writing from the publisher, except by reviewers, who may quote brief passages in a review.

ISBN: 978-0-578-90729-1

Library of Congress Control Number: 2021908977

Printed in the United States of America

YarnWhirled Press

Visit www.YarnWhirled.com

## Dedicated with love to RJ and Connor

# CONTENTS

THREAD BUTTON JEWELRY ............................................. 7
DORSET BUTTON HISTORY ............................................. 8
GETTING STARTED — THE MATERIALS ..................... 10
HOW TO CUSTOMIZE YOUR BUTTONS ..................... 13
THE FOUR STEPS OF BUTTON MAKING ................... 14
THE VARIATIONS ............................................................. 31
CONSTRUCTING THE JEWELRY ..................................... 39
THE PATTERNS ................................................................. 42
DORSET CARTWHEEL JEWELRY .................................. 44
SWANSTON BUTTON JEWELRY .................................... 58
SIMPLE SPOKE JEWELRY ................................................. 68
BLANDFORD BUTTON JEWELRY ................................... 74
OUTER RING WRAP JEWELRY ....................................... 84
SIX PETAL FLOWER JEWELRY ........................................ 94
FLOWERS & LEAVES JEWELRY ..................................... 102
POSY BUTTON JEWELRY .............................................. 108

GLOSSARY ........................................................................ 114
INDEX ................................................................................ 116

# THREAD BUTTON JEWELRY

Hand made fiber ornament is popular in many cultures around the world, from the finger knotted bracelets of Native and Central Americans, to the silk knotted cords of the Chinese, and the Kumihimo of the Japanese, the thread Jhumka of India, and the Martisor cord of Romania. The lovely British Dorset thread buttons that were sold for centuries as a practical fastener, were the inspiration for this collection of fun-to-create, and wonderful-to-wear jewelry.

# FROM USEFUL OBJECTS TO UNIQUE EMBELLISHMENTS

THE OVERWHELMING POPULARITY OF DORSET BUTTONS LAUNCHED AN INDUSTRY OF GREAT SIGNIFICANCE TO THE BRITISH ECONOMY FOR ALMOST THREE HUNDRED YEARS.

**English baby gown ca. 1800-1815.** (above) This gown features lace on the sleeves with an anchor motif, probably giving a nod to the English Navy of the period. The back closes with mismatched buttons; one with "cartwheel" threadwork and the other fabric covered with a central flower. The latter button might be a later addition; its buttonhole is oriented horizontally instead of vertically like the top buttonhole, and it is placed over a reinforcing patch that appears to have been added at a later date. **English baby gown ca. 1790-1810.** (inset opposite page) Dorset button at the shoulder measuring 11 mm.

*Both gowns are from the collection of Sara Rivers Cofield. Photography by Sara Rivers Cofield.*

As seventeenth century fashions changed to more fitted silhouettes, the need arose for a more sophisticated solution than the fabric and leather laces which had been used to hold together clothing. The invention of the Dorset thread wrapped button was met with tremendous interest, as they were not only affordable, but equally importantly, they were able to hold up admirably well to the extremely rough and punishing laundering techniques of the time.

The belief is that that the first style of Dorset button was invented in the early 1600's by a man named Abraham Case, who was a British soldier. The first buttons were made from fine wool yarn or linen cloth stitched over rings made from rams' horns, while later designs were made from linen threads that was wound over brass rings. The original workers were predominantly women and children from farming families living in Dorset County in South West England, who were able to supplement their meager family incomes by making buttons at home or at school. Some of the most industrious workers were said to have made dozens of buttons a day!

The simple tiny white buttons were often used on undergarments and shirtwaists, while the larger, more intricate versions appear to have been made for men's waistcoats, where they could be shown off to their greatest advantage. The buttons, which were sewn onto colored cards, were shipped all over Europe, the United States and Canada, and as far away as Australia.

With all of the gorgeous threads that we have at our disposal today, we can construct colorful variations that draw their inspiration from the classic techniques of the original buttoners. And, fortunately, we are no longer limited to making buttons merely as a way to fasten our clothing: we can enjoy them for the amazing little adornments that they are, too.

The very easy to learn wrapping techniques that are key parts of Dorset button making are useful and enjoyable additions to any modern crafter's repertoire. Buttons take a small amount of fiber so they are really quite economical to construct. Hand wrapped thread buttons will enhance every one of your embroidery, quilting, knitting, crocheting, sewing, tatting, weaving, paper-craft, woodwork, metal work, bookbinding and jewelry projects—and, yes, they keep clothing closed, very well, indeed.

The original pieceworkers would be amazed at the current interest in their work. They probably could not have envisioned a world where their hard labor would be considered an art to be practiced as a pastime, and that their handcrafted objects would be looked upon with wonder. Creating Dorset buttons to use for jewelry making spans a perfect bridge between traditional craft and contemporary art. Make one, whether it is a classic *Cartwheel* button or a modern iteration like the *Outer Wrap Ring* button, and you will feel the additional satisfaction of knowing that you are helping to keep a heritage world craft tradition alive.

# GETTING STARTED – The Materials

ONE OF THE BEST THINGS ABOUT THREAD JEWELRY MAKING IS THAT IT ONLY REQUIRES A VERY FEW EASY TO OBTAIN SUPPLIES.

Thread jewelry making is a wonderfully portable craft, and even the most elaborate buttons are not expensive to make. Don't worry if you are unable to find the same rings or threads that are called for in each pattern. Any project from this book can be adapted to a large variety of rings or threads, just by adjusting the number of *Cast Knots, Laid Spokes, and Rounding* in the pattern so that it will suit your own personal choice of materials.

## Rings

Most of the examples in this book are made over widely available plastic rings which are produced for garment and curtain making. Metal rings are fine, as long as they have been soldered closed and are formed of a non rusting alloy. Use a small file or emery board to gently sand any imperfections on the surface of the ring. The ring size used for the sample shown is specified in each pattern, but, remember, it is merely a guideline.

Rings can vary greatly. The outer dimension size in each pattern is given as an example, but note that the inner dimension of a ring may be a different size, so your button may look different, or may require more or less rounding than the pattern calls for.

## Needles

A needle with a large eye and a blunt tip such as a large size tapestry needle is used for almost every step of the button making process, from the casting and anchoring, to the laying and rounding. Surprisingly enough, the tapestry needle is not used for stitching— it provides weight and something to grip, so that you will not experience hand fatigue from pinching the fine thread during the casting step. You may knot the tapestry needle onto the end of your thread so it won't slide off while you are working. The blunt tip of a tapestry needle will ensure that you won't poke your fingers while you are *Rounding* the button.

During the *Laying and Rounding* steps the chenille needle (which has a large eye and a pointed tip), is used to secure the threads to the work, because it can pierce the threads on the back of the button. Once the initial threads have been secured on, switch back to a tapestry needle for the rest of the *Laying* and *Rounding* steps, so you don't prick your hand.

The projects in this book were constructed with a size 16 tapestry needle and a size 18 chenille needle. A selection of smaller size needles is necessary for finer threads and tinier rings, and other needles, such as embroidery needles are useful if you plan to embellish your buttons with embroidery stitches.

## Scissors

A small pair of scissors with pointed tips is necessary so that you can clip the threads very closely to the button ring. Don't use your best pair of embroidery scissors to cut real metallic threads— the presence of metal in the threads can cause your scissor blades to nick and dull.

## Threads

Selecting the threads is the fun part. Buttons only take a few yards of thread, so this is a great chance to enjoy trying a new fiber, or to use threads from your stash. Suggested thread yardage amounts have been included in each pattern. You may find that you need more or less thread than the pattern calls for—it is always better to have extra on hand. Keep in mind that although you can use a more fragile fiber for the *Rounding* step, the *Casting* and *Laying* steps require a firmer, stronger thread.

### Cotton

Pearl Cotton is a lustrous, highly mercerized, two ply non-divisible thread that is available in sizes 3, 5, 8, and 12, which are sold in balls or in twisted hanks. It is one of my favorite fibers for thread jewelry making. All of the button samples in this book were made from DMC *Article #115 Pearl Cotton size 5.*

Six Strand Cotton Floss is easy to find, inexpensive, and it comes in an amazing variety of colors. Embroidery floss will "spread" more than a non-divisible thread, so it will provide a good coverage, and a soft finish. Four strands of six strand embroidery floss are relatively comparable in size to one piece of Pearl Cotton #5. One strand of cotton Floche is very suitable for button making as well.

### Wool

Divisible plied tapestry yarn which is sold in cut pieces and hanks, finer crewel wools, lace weight and fingering yarn are all perfect for button making. The sturdier wools will not pill as much as the softer fibers will.

### Linen/Flax

The Dorset buttons from the 17th and 18th century were constructed primarily from native hemp and flax/linen fibers. Select a simple button pattern to really highlight linen's mild sheen, richness, and depth.

### Silk

Silk fibers are strong, inelastic, take dye just beautifully, and possess a luminous and a nearly reflective quality. Jewelry is lovely in silk, as it is not subject to too much wear and tear. Work with shorter lengths of silk thread to minimize the chance of fraying.

### Novelty and Metallic Fibers

There are multiple synthetics, leather, metallics, and rayon (pulp) fibers available, all of which have different properties and textures. All of the metallic threads used in this book are either DMC *Diamant or Diamant Grandé*, which, respectively, are about the diameter of one or two strands of embroidery floss. Novelty fibers may used to great effect to cover an entire button or as an accent. Buttons are an ideal small "canvas" on which to experiment!

#  HOW TO CUSTOMIZE YOUR BUTTONS

HERE ARE A FEW SIMPLE PATTERN ADJUSTMENTS THAT WILL HELP YOU CONSTRUCT A BUTTON THAT IS UNIQUELY YOURS.

One of the best parts of making thread wrapped buttons is being able to try out different fibers and different size rings. Any of the button and jewelry patterns in this book can be modified. And, luckily, it is an easy enough matter to make substitutions: all that you will need to do is to use the information on this page to adapt one or all of the basic steps to suit your button. It may take some experimentation. If you cover the button ring completely with *Cast Knots*, and *lay* all of the spokes evenly, you should be fine. The patterns in this book give the amounts used to create the examples in the photographs.

**Number of Cast Knots**
Make as many *Cast Knots* as you need so that your button ring is completely covered. If you are feeling gutsy, then just cover the ring with *Cast Knots* until it is full, and then estimate the distance in between to *lay* each spoke: that is how the original makers made their buttons. If you like more precision, and plan to count the *Cast Knots* in between spokes during the *Laying* step, make sure that the number of *Cast Knots* you make is a multiple of the number of spokes you plan to *lay*. For example, if the pattern calls for 72 *Cast Knots* and 12 *Laid Spokes* (each spoke placed 6 *Cast Knots* apart), and your own thread/ring selection will require approximately 100 *Cast Knots* to cover your ring, if you make 96 *Cast Knots* (8x12=96) then you will be able to *lay* 12 spokes with 8 *Cast Knots* in between each spoke. Alternatively, you could make 108 *Cast Knots* (9 x12=108) and you could *lay* each of the 12 spokes 9 *Cast Knots* apart.

**Number of Laid Spokes**
Depending upon your own supplies, you may need to add or subtract spokes during the *Laying* step. The *Blandford* button, and the *Dorset Cartwheel* button are both great buttons to start out with if you want to change the number of *Laid Spokes*, as any number of spokes will work. The *Swanston* button in this book uses a number of spokes that is divisible by four, so you would have to plan ahead accordingly.

**Number of Rounds**
You may find that you need to adjust the number of rounds needed to complete your button, depending upon the weight of your thread, the size of your rings, or your own working tension. Make as many rounds as necessary to make your button beautiful—the number of rounds is absolutely up to you. If you are making a more intricate pattern, try to add or subtract during the simple rounds.

# THE FOUR STEPS OF BUTTON MAKING

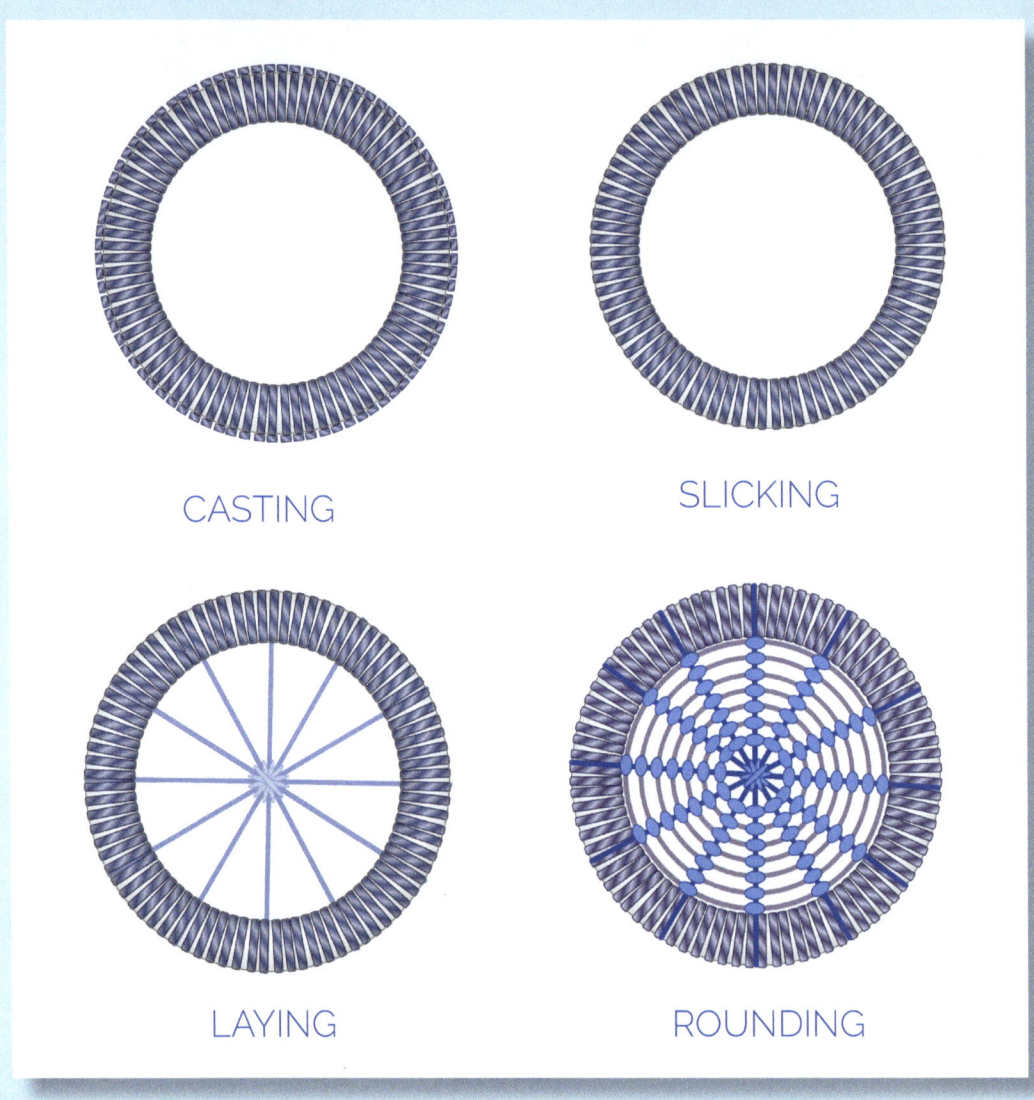

CASTING

SLICKING

LAYING

ROUNDING

The crafters who enjoy creating Dorset buttons in the twenty-first century still make use of the same four easy-to-master techniques which the original piecework button makers plied hundreds of years ago: *Casting, Slicking, Laying, and Rounding*. The patterns at the end of this book are based upon those four traditional methods, with my own addition of *Anchoring* as its own separate step. Although the first button makers learned from spoken directions, and by copying others, the instructions on the next few pages have clear step by step illustrations so that you may find this wonderful needle art to be as easy to master as possible.

Although button making may be unfamiliar to you, I am confident that you will find it to be enjoyable once you have mastered each step. The instructions are meant to guide you through this heritage craft, one technique at a time. At the beginning of every grouping of buttons, I have included an illustration of a completed button, both for those who would prefer to see a diagram and keep going without written directions, as well as for those who like to have visual reinforcement. All of the illustrations, except when specifically noted, are drawn so that you are looking at the front of the button. I have written the patterns giving the precise information that I used to create the buttons that are pictured on the pattern pages. But every crafter has their own way of working and it is important to know that buttonmaking does not have to be an exact science. Follow the prescribed steps once, and you will understand how simple it is to adapt *Casting, Slicking, Laying, and Rounding* to make more buttons, in any manner, or with any materials that you choose.

In their heyday, it is said that piecework button makers could make an average of 7 dozen buttons a day. The buttons that are used in jewelry making are much larger and many are more complex, so I am perfectly content if I can fit in the time to make one or two in a day, and you should be, too. All of the jewelry in this book was constructed using rings that were covered with *Cast Knots* made out of thread. Even the most simple *Cast rings* can be used to make a pretty piece of jewelry. Persevere, and learn how to complete the *Laying* and the *Rounding* steps, and you will be amazed at the infinite variety of patterns that you can create.

# SUGGESTIONS

- The diagrams depict each individual step in a different color. But, if you craft your first button with one continuous length of thread, you won't have to begin and end new threads. If you find the long thread tricky to manage, or if you wish to change colors, you can try to use shorter pieces of thread for each one of the *Casting, Laying, Anchoring,* and *Rounding* steps.

- If you knot the thread on to the tapestry needle it will not fall off, and it is definitely easier to manage. Any knot, such as an overhand knot or Lark's head knot is fine. The needle is not shown to be knotted onto the thread in the diagrams for simplicity, but I do knot it on when I am making a button.

- If you need to switch threads, just thread the chenille needle with the new thread, and anchor the thread to the back of the button, right underneath the *Anchoring* stitches or beneath the ring, by knotting or weaving it into one of the *Cast Knot* "bumps" until it is attached firmly. Once you have secured the thread, use sharp scissors to clip the thread end.

- I switch back and forth between a tapestry needle and a chenille needle. This is optional, but I like the tapestry needle for its weight, and the fact that it does not split the threads, and I use the chenille needle to attach a new thread, or to secure a thread that I am finished using. I unknot the thread, remove the tapestry needle, and place the chenille needle on the thread. I do not knot the thread onto the chenille needle since I use that needle to weave or sew through other threads.

- Secure a thread it in place by making a few back stitches or small knots into the *Cast Knots* on the back of the ring.

- Learning how to control the thread can be tricky. **If your thread begins to twist, stand up and** drop the threaded needle from your hand, and allow the needle to dangle and spin until the thread untwists completely.

- If a thread is very twisty, it may help to start fresh, and to try switching the direction that you are working from clockwise to counterclockwise. Threads have their own twist, and some threads respond better if you change the way that you wrap them.

# STEP 1–CASTING

DURING THE CASTING STEP, THE RING IS COVERED WITH CAST KNOTS MADE OUT OF THREAD. CAST KNOTS IN DORSET BUTTON MAKING ARE CREATED IN A VERY SIMILAR MANNER TO HALF HITCHES IN MACRAMÉ, AND BLANKET STITCHES IN EMBROIDERY.

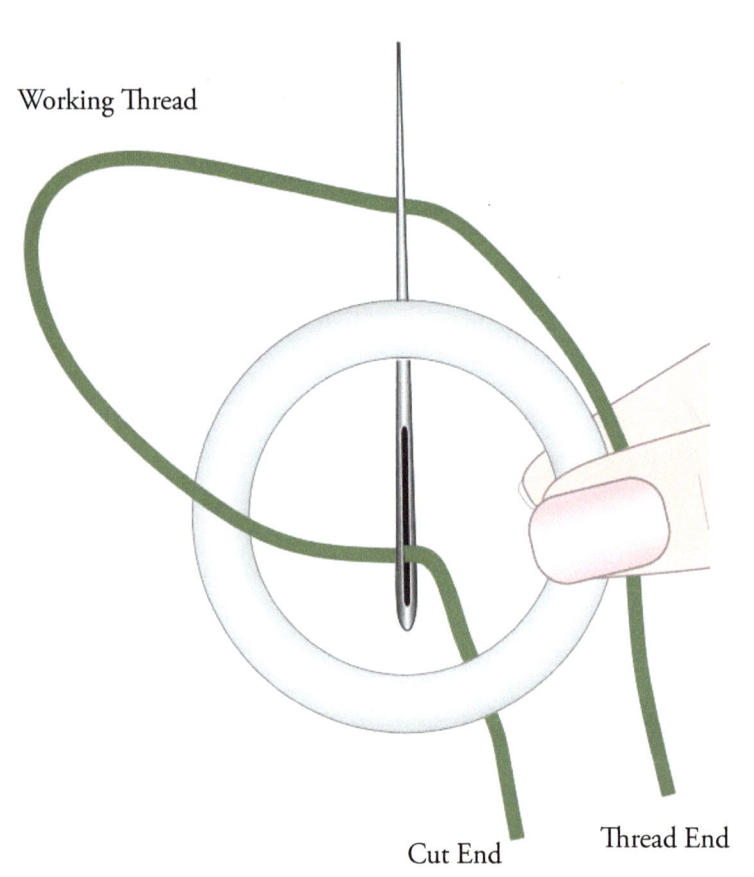

Working Thread

Cut End    Thread End

It is easier to work the *Casting* step if you tie the last couple of inches of the cut end of the thread onto the needle, so that the needle cannot fall off of the thread. Any type of knot will work. The end of the thread by the eye of the needle will be referred to as the **cut end (which can be knotted onto the needle)**, and the length of thread (which can be quite long) will be referred to as the **working thread**. The absolute bottom part of the working thread will be referred to as the **thread end.**

### How to Make the First Cast Knot

To cover a 1 inch/ 2.5 cm diameter button ring, thread a size 16 tapestry needle with a 2 yard/1.8 m piece of thread in a weight similar to a Pearl Cotton #5 or a Six Strand Embroidery floss. Attach the thread to the ring by pinching the lower couple of inches of the working thread and the ring together, and then make the *Cast Knots* over both the ring and the thread as follows: insert the threaded needle from the front to behind the ring, so that the pointed end of the needle lands in between the ring and loop formed by the working thread. Pull on the needle gently until the thread is flush against the ring- 1 *Cast Knot* made. Note that when the needle is behind the ring, it must be between the ring and the thread in order to make the knot.

**P**ull very gently on the *Cast Knots* as you work, so that they are uniform in size. The knots will wind up getting pushed to the back of your work eventually, so don't worry if they don't seem to be all lined up perfectly at the outer edge of the ring. Aim for a smooth and even tension, and try to cover the ring completely.

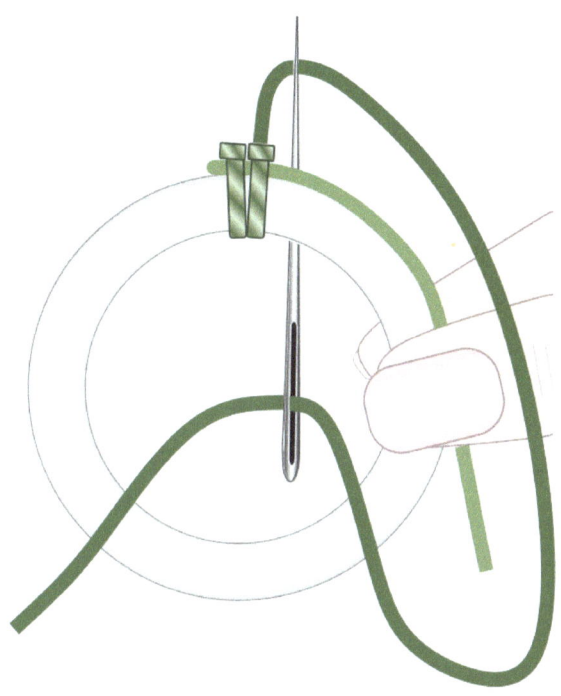

THE FIRST FEW KNOTS ARE TRICKY, BUT YOU WILL QUICKLY BECOME ACCUSTOMED TO MANAGING THE EXTREMELY LONG LENGTHS OF THREAD.

**S**ince ring sizes and thread weights (even among different colors of the same thread) can vary, you may find that you need to make more or fewer *Cast Knots* to cover your own ring. If you change the number of *Cast Knots* called for in the pattern, keep in mind that during the *Laying* step you might need to adjust the amount of *Cast Knots* in between each spoke that you make.

### SUBSEQUENT CAST KNOTS

Continue to cover the rest of the ring with *Cast Knots* following the instructions for the first *Cast Knot*, by inserting the threaded needle into the ring from the front to the back, exiting through the loop that is then formed by the working thread.

### COVERING THE THREAD END

In the illustration above, the first few *Cast Knots* cover the last few inches of the working thread, which will bury the thread end under the work, and make it more secure. Once you have worked over at least 1 inch/2.5 cm of the thread end, you may clip the rest of it close to the surface of the ring. If you find that it is too difficult to work over the working thread end, then start the first cast knot by temporarily knotting the thread to the ring. You can weave this end in later.

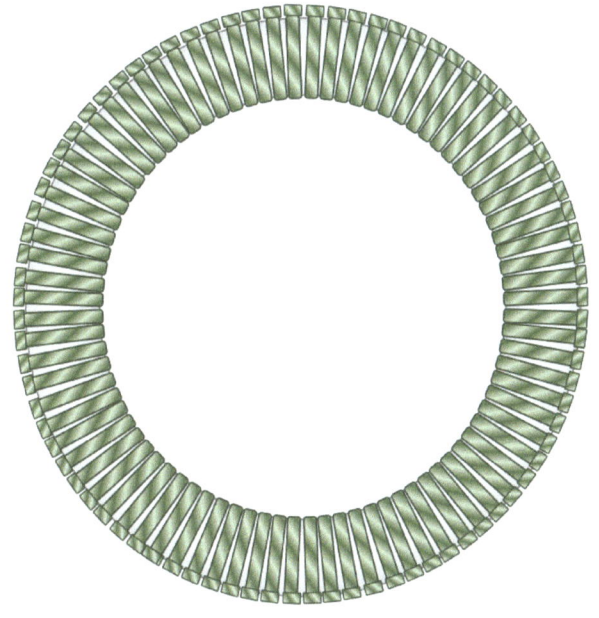

A Ring With 84 Cast Knots

# STEP 2 – SLICKING

IN THE SLICKING STEP, ALL OF THE RIDGED BUMPS ON THE OUTSIDE OF THE RING ARE GENTLY NUDGED TO THE UNDERSIDE OF THE RING.

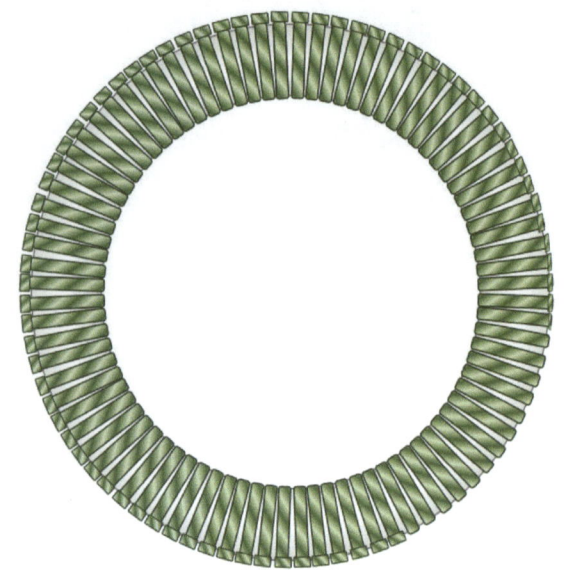

Slicking in Progress

## How to Slick the Ring

(Note that the needle is still attached for this step.) Using your index finger, gently push all of the ridged bumps that are along the outer edge of the ring to the underside of the ring, where they will not be visible from the front. It is important not to push them so far that they migrate to the inside edge of the ring. The bottom right of the diagram to the left shows a neatly slicked edge.

AS YOU CONTINUE WITH THE NEXT FEW STEPS, YOU MIGHT NOTICE THAT SOME OF THE KNOTS OCASSIONALLY BEGIN TO MIGRATE BACK TOWARDS THE INNER OR OUTER EDGE OF THE RING, SO BE PREPARED TO KEEP NUDGING THEM BACK INTO PLACE BEHIND THE RING.

In the patterns on the following pages, a ring that has been covered with *Cast Knot*s and that has been slicked is referred to as a *Cast ring*. The knots, or "bumps" on the back of any ring are an ideal place to attach a new piece of thread or to bury the end of a thread that you are finished using.

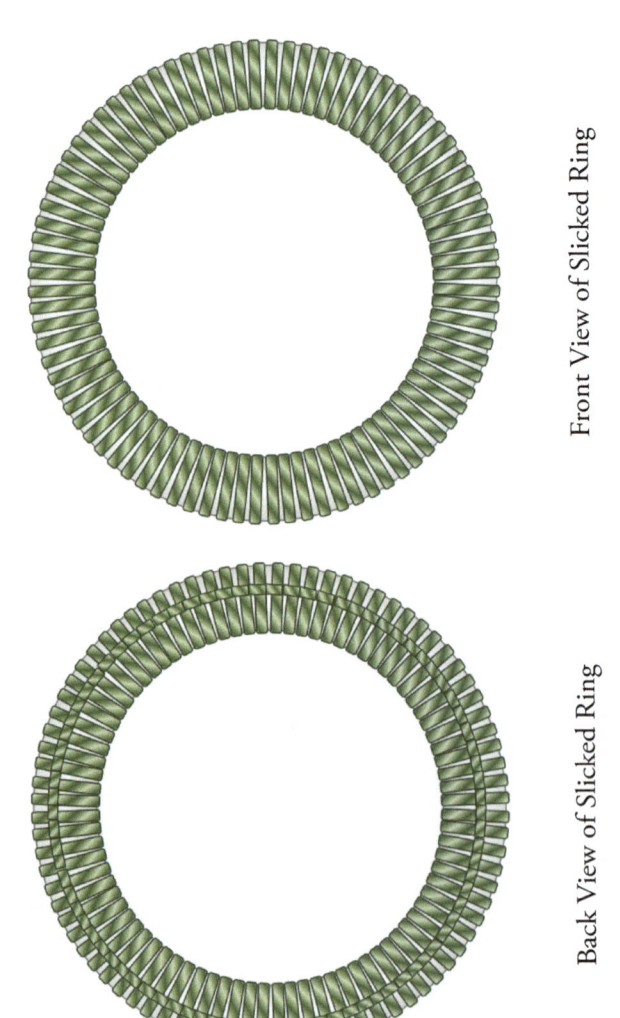

Front View of Slicked Ring

Back View of Slicked Ring

# SECURING THE THREAD

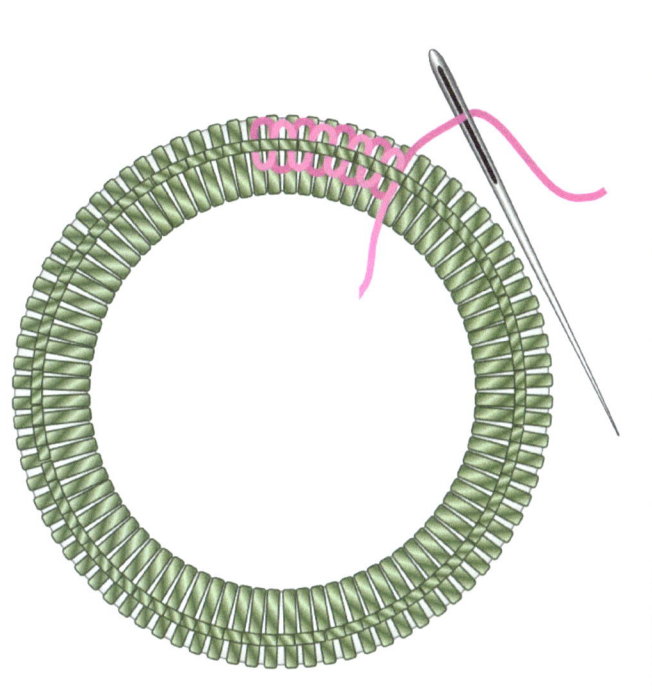

I know that it is counterintuitive for most needleworkers to knot any threads on the back of their work, but for button making it is really necessary to make sure that the threads will not become undone. It is much more important that the threads are very firmly attached and not visible from the front, than it is for the back to look lovely. Certain threads are more slippery than others: in particular metallic, rayon, and silk fibers may need extra fastening behind the ring. If you think a piece of thread might need to be further secured, you may put a drop of acid free glue on top of the knot. But, beware, because the glue may leave a stiff area behind your button which might not be an issue for a drop earring, but might be quite uncomfortable to wear directly against your skin in a necklace or a bracelet.

BUTTON MAKING FIBERS NEED TO BE FIRMLY ATTACHED, SO STITCH A GENEROUS LENGTH OF THE THREAD
IN AND OUT OF THE CAST KNOTS ON THE BACK OF THE RING, AS SHOWN ABOVE, OR USE A STRONG KNOT TO SECURE ANY LOOSE ENDS

The phrase **"Secure and clip the thread"** is used throughout this book, to indicate that the thread you are using should be knotted or woven in, into an unobtrusive place behind the button or the ring, until it has been fastened thoroughly. Turn the button over so that the underside of the button is facing you. If you are changing threads, you may need to begin or end a new thread behind the wraps in the center of the button from the *Anchoring* step. Sometimes it easier to finish the entire button and then find a spot to weave the ends in later. The phrase **"Switch to color __ thread"** implies that the previous thread has been secured and clipped first.

You may wish to switch to a chenille needle. Weave the threaded needle in and out of the ridged bumps a number of times, switching directions halfway through, or stitch a few back stitches or embroider or tie a few knots to secure the tail. Clip the thread close to the surface of the button. If you do not clip the thread close to the button, the tail may wind up on the front of the button.

# STEP 3A—LAYING THE SPOKES

DURING THE LAYING STEP, THREAD IS WOUND OVER AND UNDER ACROSS THE DIAMETER OF THE RING TO FORM SPOKES, WHICH ARE PLACED IN BETWEEN CAST KNOTS FOR SECURITY.

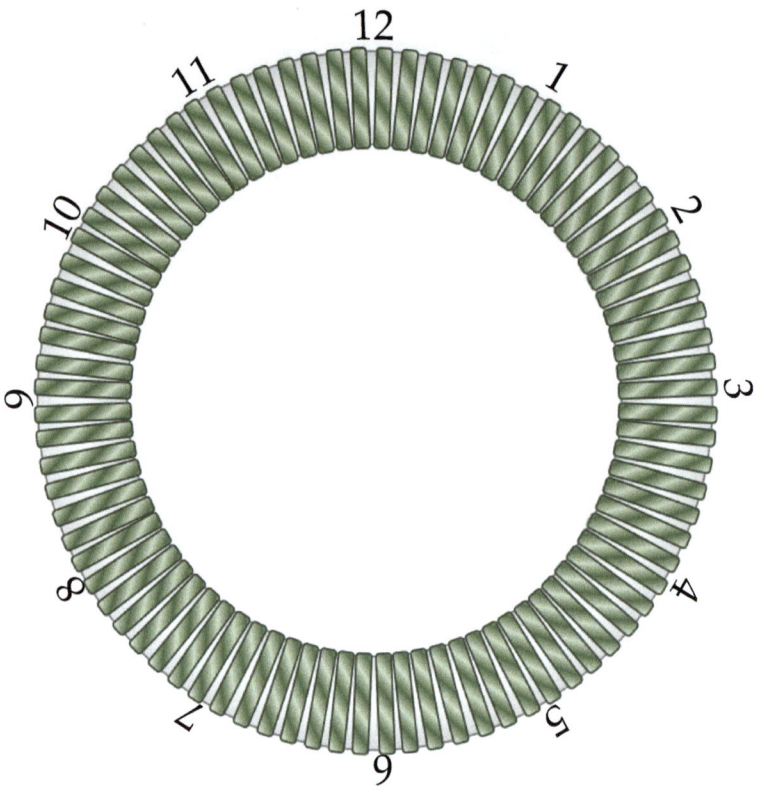

Cast ring marked with the positions of twelve imaginary spokes

### TIPS

- For many of the buttons shown in this book, such as the *Dorset Cartwheel* or the *Blandford* button, the number of spokes that you *lay* is entirely your choice. Keep the weight of the thread and the size of the ring in mind. The example shows a 12 spoke button, which is easy for most beginners to visualize, because the spokes will be *laid* in the exact same positions as the numbers on a clock. The directions will refer to these positions by referencing the clock points. For most beginners, *laying* eight spokes is also easy: picture slices of pizza in a pizza pie.

- Spacing the spokes an equal distance apart will make it easier in the next step to *anchor* them exactly in the middle so that you can *round* your button evenly.

- It is also helpful to *lay* the top spokes firmly in between each cast knot, rather than having them sit above the *Cast Knots*.

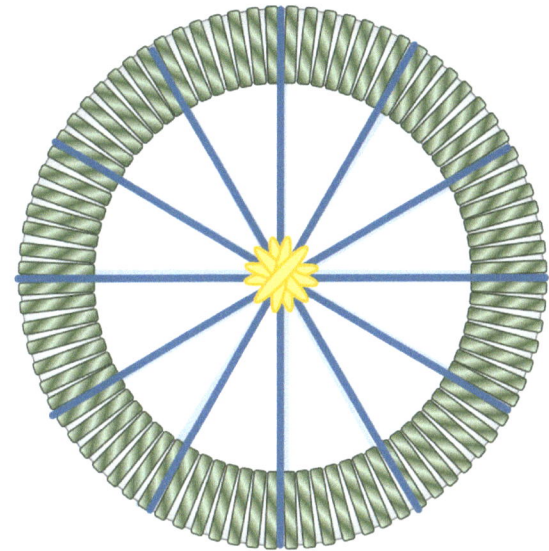

Counting the *Cast Knots* and *laying* the threads in between equal amounts of *Cast Knots* will yield a button that will replicate the sample button in each picture, and for that reason, each pattern lists the amount of *Cast Knots* in between each *laid* spoke. However, if you are more relaxed, or gutsy, and just want to estimate the distance between each *laid* spoke go ahead and do so, knowing that you are in the fine company of all of the buttonmakers who came before you, and who at an unnerving production rate of dozens of buttons a day, certainly couldn't have been bothered by the persnickety task of counting each knot. Either method will work, whether you opt to count each *Cast Knot*, or whether you prefer to *lay* each spoke in an approximate position, you will still have a beautiful button at the end.

---

TAKE A DEEP BREATH.
LAYING THE SPOKES BECOMES
SO MUCH EASIER WITH JUST A
LITTLE BIT OF PRACTICE.

---

- **Every spoke is made up of a pair of coordinating threads,** with one thread beneath the ring, and one thread on top of the ring. In the illustrations, the top threads are shown in dark blue, and the underneath threads are shown in a lighter blue.

- It is crucial to start each pair of spokes by wrapping the thread from the first point to the second point **underneath** the ring, and then *lay* the top thread of the spoke **over the top** of the ring, from the second point on the ring back to the first point. Otherwise you may wind up with a top single spoke, which will make the *Rounding* step more difficult. This is true for all of the button patterns in this book.

- During the *Laying* step **only the first spoke** (12 o'clock to 6 o'clock, and then back from 6 o'clock to 12 o'clock) **will have the top and bottom threads in the same position**: for all of the other spokes, the top thread will be correctly situated, and the bottom thread will be the thread which "travels," so it will be situated at an angle to the top thread. It is only once all of the spokes have been *laid*, and have been *anchored* in the center, that the top and bottom threads will be corralled together in pairs, and each spoke will have a clearly visible top and bottom thread.

- **You must have a top and at least one bottom thread for each spoke.** Depending upon how you finish your thread once you have completed your last spoke, you may notice that ½ of one spoke (a radius) has 2 "bottom threads." That is perfectly fine—just remember that you need to treat those two bottom threads as if they were one thread when you get to the *Rounding* step.

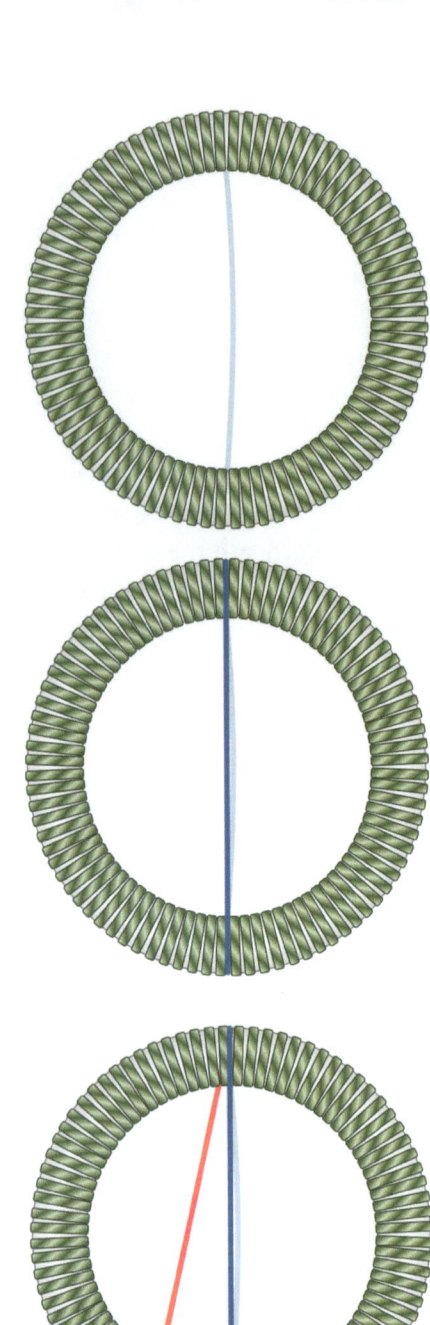

### Laying the First Spoke

**01** Start at the 12 o'clock position. Working below the ring, bring the thread from the 12 o'clock position to the 6 o'clock position.

### Laying the Second Spoke

**02** Start at the 6 o'clock position. Working above the ring, bring the thread from the 6 o'clock position to the 12 o'clock position.

### Laying the Third Spoke

**03** Start at the 12 o'clock position. Working below the ring, bring the thread from the 12 o'clock position to the 7 o'clock position.

### Laying the Fourth Spoke

**04** Start at the 7 o'clock position. Working above the ring, bring the thread from the 7 o'clock position to the 1 o'clock position.

## Laying the Fifth Spoke

Start at the 1 o'clock position. Working below the ring, bring the thread from the 1 o'clock position to the 8 o'clock position.

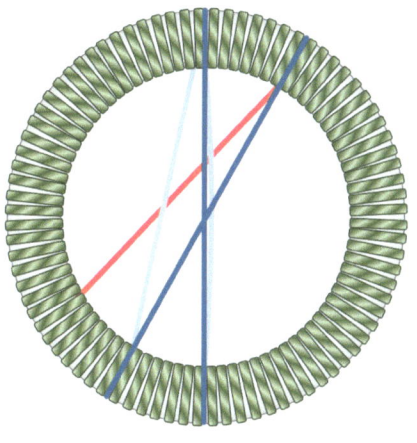

## Laying the Sixth Spoke

Start at the 8 o'clock position. Working above the ring, bring the thread from the 8 o'clock position to the 2 o'clock position.

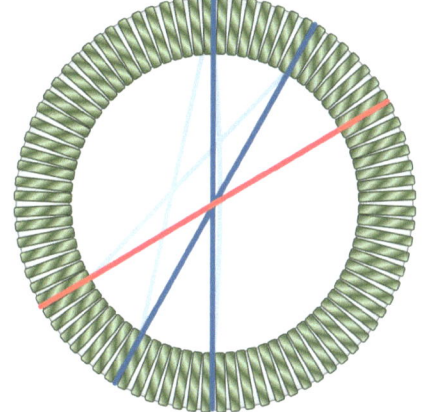

## Laying the Seventh Spoke

Start at the 2 o'clock position. Working below the ring, bring the thread from the 2 o'clock position to the 9 o'clock position.

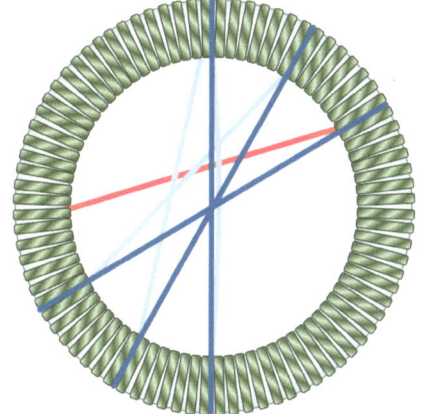

## Laying the Eighth Spoke

Start at the 9 o'clock position. Working above the ring, bring the thread from the 9 o'clock position to the 3 o'clock position.

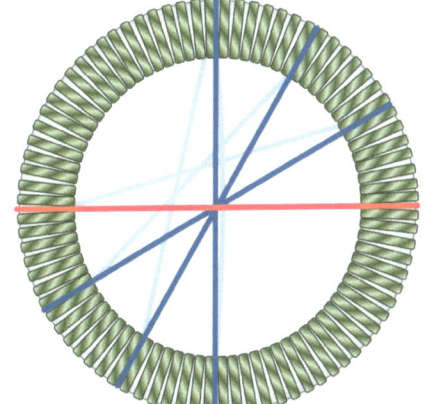

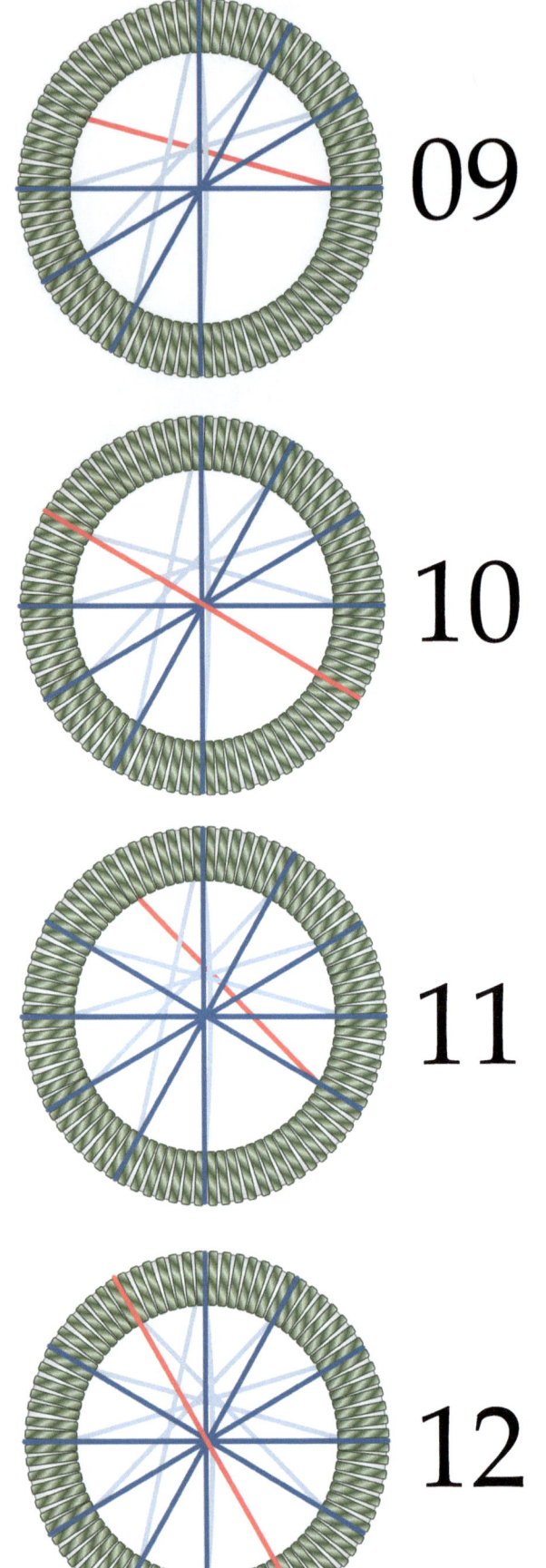

## Laying the Ninth Spoke

Start at the 3 o'clock position. Working below the ring, bring the thread from the 3 o'clock position to the 10 o'clock position.

## Laying the Tenth Spoke

Start at the 10 o'clock position. Working above the ring, bring the thread from the 10 o'clock position to the 4 o'clock position.

## Laying the Eleventh Spoke

Start at the 4 o'clock position. Working below the ring, bring the thread from the 4 o'clock position to the 11 o'clock position.

## Laying the Twelfth Spoke

Start at the 11 o'clock position. Working above the ring, bring the thread from the 11 o'clock position to the 5 o'clock position.

# Laying the Final Thread to Complete the Spokes

## *The Final Thread*

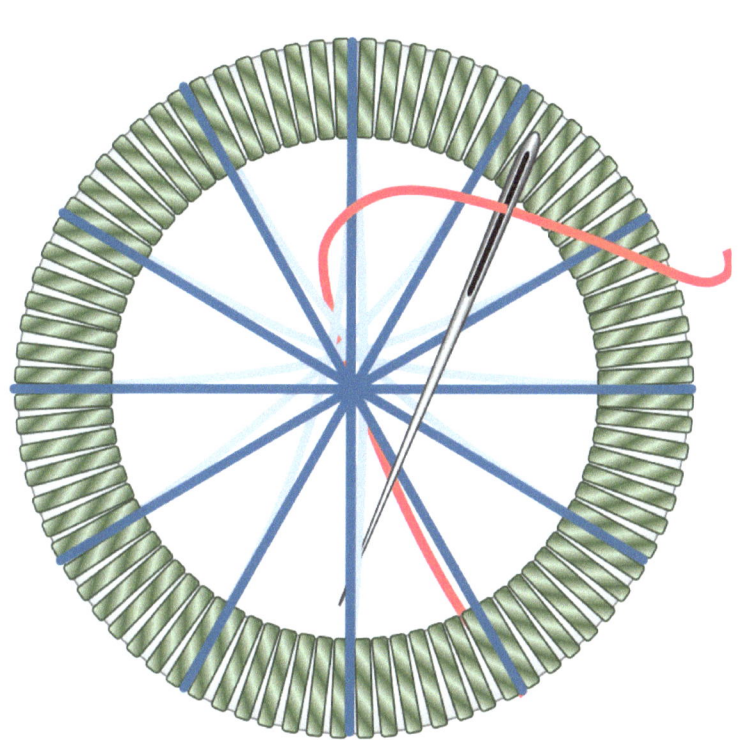

This very important step fills in the missing underneath thread for the last *Laid Spoke,* aligns all of the underneath and top spokes, and also places the threaded needle into the correct spot to begin the next step, which is the *Anchoring* step. Completing the last spoke in this manner is really necessary, because in order to be able to properly cover the spokes during the *Rounding* step, every top spoke needs to have its own coordinating bottom spoke. The red thread on the diagram below shows the path of the last spoke.

The final underneath thread is *laid* after all of the other spokes have been *laid*. The last *Laid Spoke* should be on top of the ring, and the position where it ends will be the starting point for this step. In this example, the last *Laid Spoke* (the twelfth spoke on page 26) ended on top of the ring with the threaded needle at the 5 o'clock position.

Bring the threaded needle underneath the ring and carry it below the center of all of the spokes. Emerge to the front of the button in the space in between the 11 and 12 o'clock spokes, capturing the nexus (the spot where all of the threads meet in the center) of all of the threads. Pull gently on the spokes to align them, and then bring the threaded needle through to the back in the space in between the 5 and 6 o'clock spokes.

# STEP 3B—ANCHORING THE LAID SPOKES

IN THE **ANCHORING** STEP ALL OF THE **LAID SPOKES** ARE GATHERED AND HELD TOGETHER IN THE MIDDLE BY A NUMBER OF WRAPS WHICH SERVE TO KEEP THE SPOKES ALIGNED AND CENTERED.

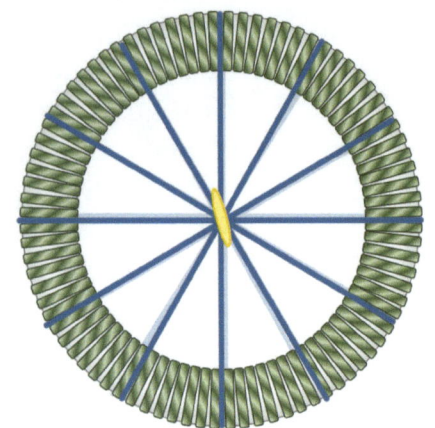

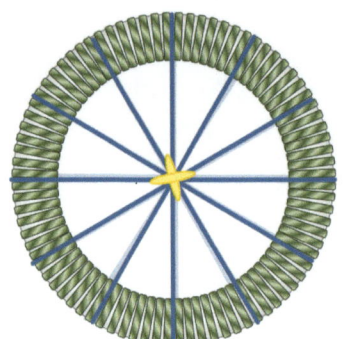

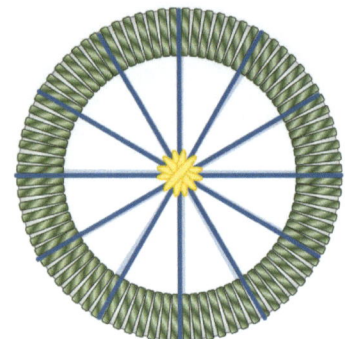

### Step 1—Align and Secure the Spokes

Start with the threaded needle on the top of the button in between the 5 o'clock and 6 o'clock spokes, then insert the threaded needle into the space between the 11 o'clock and the 12 o'clock spokes, pulling it behind the button, and, tugging very gently to align the spokes.

### Step 2—Anchor the rest of the spokes in a Criss Cross Fashion.

Using the threaded needle, wrap the thread firmly around the junction of the spokes, being sure to catch both the bottom and the top thread of each spoke, making as many wraps as necessary to hold the spokes together as firmly as possible in the center of the ring. Anchor and center the spokes in the middle with a few straight wraps (forming a "+" and then an "x", repeating as needed, in a clockwise fashion) to secure. It is crucial to anchor the threads as close to the center of the circle as possible, or your finished button will not be even.

### TIPS

- It is extremely critical to *anchor* the threads firmly in the exact center of the button so that it will look balanced, and so that it will be easier to do the *Rounding* step later. Place the button flat on an even surface, and gently nudge the spokes into place before securing them in the middle.

- Some variations, such as the *Blandford* button, do not require any gathering in the center, and so the pattern will not have an *Anchoring* step.

- It is a good idea to anchor the center of the spokes with a couple of wraps using the same thread that you used to lay the spokes, even if you plan to switch to a thread of a different color for the *Anchoring* step. Secure the first thread carefully behind the button, and then clip the thread end. Thread a chenille needle with the new color thread, and attach it behind the center of the button.

# STEP 4—ROUNDING

IN THE **ROUNDING** STEP, SOME OR ALL OF THE SPOKES ARE FILLED IN BY ENCIRCLING THEM WITH THREAD. THIS TRADITIONAL METHOD WILL BE REFERRED TO AS THE **SINGLE DORSET CARTWHEEL WRAP** WHEN YOU WRAP THE THREAD OVER ONE SPOKE AT A TIME.

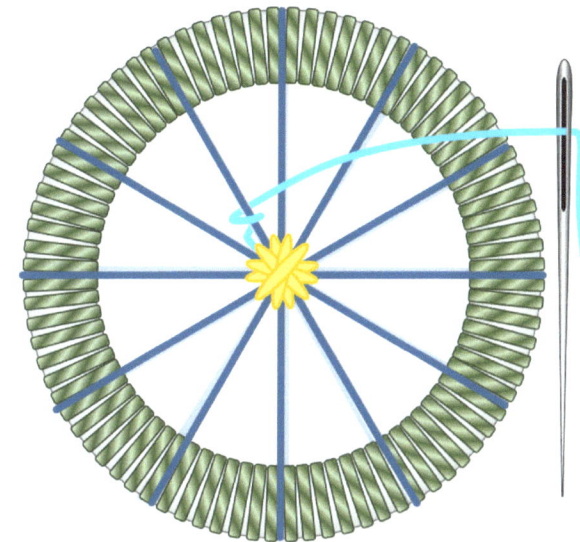

### The First Wrap

1. Bring the threaded needle up from behind the button, close to the center of the ring, to the right of the first spoke (the 11 o'clock spoke in the illustration).
2. Carry the threaded needle over and to the left of the first spoke, inserting it down into the space between that spoke (11 o'clock) and the one to its immediate left (10 o'clock), and then carry it behind the initial spoke (first single wrap made).

### All Subsequent Wraps

*Come up from behind to the right of the (next) spoke, carry the thread over that spoke, and then insert the needle down into the space to the left of the spoke (single wrap made). Repeat from * making a single wrap over each individual spokes, moving from spoke to spoke in a clockwise direction, until all of the spokes have been covered (1 round completed).

Start each new round right next to the previous round. Repeat the round as many times as necessary until the entire button is filled. Do not pull the thread too tightly, and try to maintain an even tension for best coverage. When the spokes are all filled, secure and clip the thread.

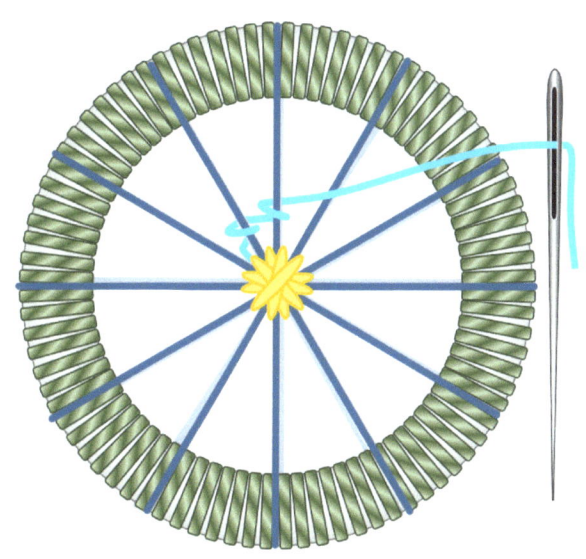

THREE ROUNDS OF THE **SINGLE DORSET CARTWHEEL WRAP** WORKED IN A CLOCKWISE DIRECTION.

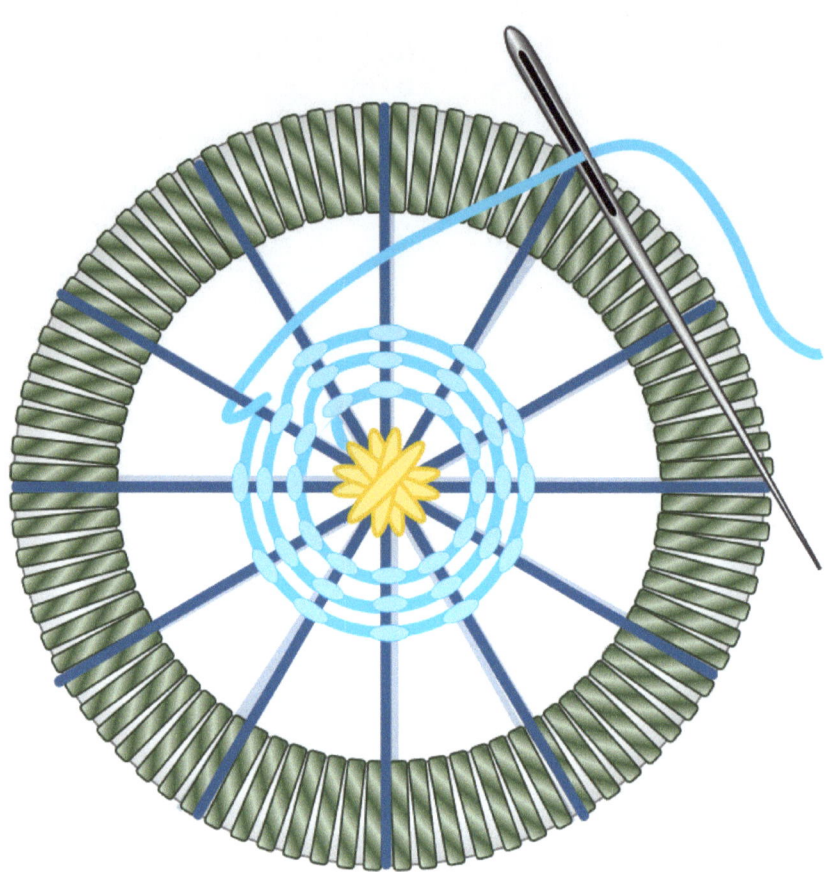

### TIPS

- *Rounding* is essentially the same as working an embroidered raised spider web/daisy stitch, or, as it is referred to in weaving, a continual soumak stitch.

- Maintain a comfortable and even tension, so that you don't distort the spokes.

- It doesn't matter if you work in a clockwise or counter clockwise direction if you are filling in an entire button with *Single Dorset Cartwheel Wraps*, as long as you are consistent and work the entire round in the same direction.

- If you change colors for the *Rounding* step, fasten the new thread on behind the anchored wraps in the center of the ring, so that your thread will be in the right position for the first round.

- Some buttons, such as the *Simple Spoke* button do not require any *Rounding*.

# THE VARIATIONS

# VARIATION 1: SINGLE DORSET CARTWHEEL WRAP WORKED OVER A PAIR OF SPOKES

During the *Rounding* step, a *Single Dorset Cartwheel Wrap Worked over a Pair of Spokes* is made when the working thread goes around two spokes (both the top and bottom threads) at the same time, encircling them completely. This simple version is worked in the same way as the *Single Dorset Cartwheel Wrap*, except that you will be covering two spokes at the same time, with a single wrap.

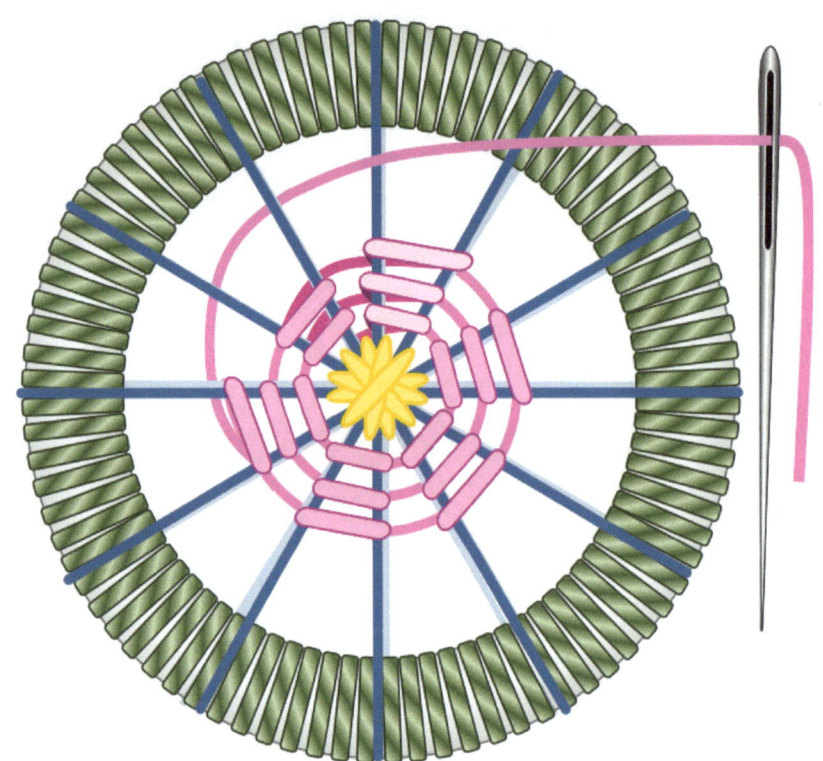

**SINGLE DORSET CARTWHEEL WRAP WORKED OVER A PAIR OF SPOKES**

In this example, the 12 spoke button pictured above has 6 pairs of spokes, numbered as if on a clock [12-1, 2-3, 4-5, 6-7, 8-9, 10-11].
*Working in a clockwise fashion, bring the threaded needle from behind the button up through the space to the right of the first pair of spokes (12-1); next, carry the threaded needle over the top of the same pair of spokes and insert the needle into the space to the left of that pair of spokes; finally, slide the threaded needle beneath the pair of spokes (2-3) that is to the immediate right of the pair of spokes (12-1) that was just covered—one *Single Dorset Cartwheel Wrap Over a Pair of Spokes* completed. Repeat from * covering each of the remaining pairs of spokes to complete the round. Make sure to capture both the top and bottom thread of each spoke.

# VARIATION 2: REVERSE CARTWHEEL WRAP

For this traditional variation of the *Dorset Cartwheel Wrap*, the working thread will cover two spokes, and it is wrapped from the top, then under and around one spoke. The top of this button has the appearance of the underside of a *Dorset Cartwheel* wrapped button.

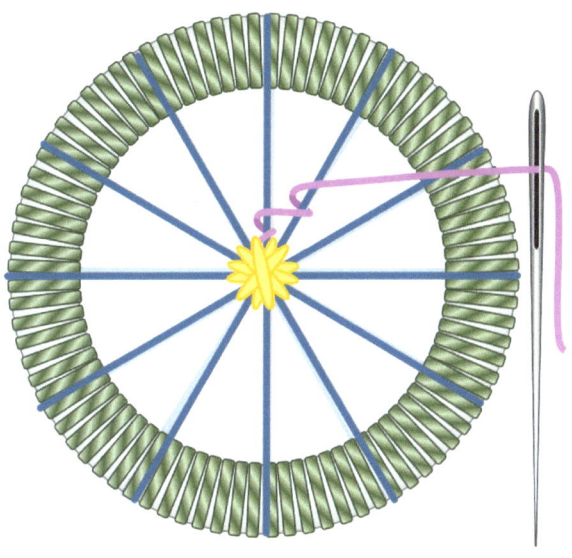

One Reverse Cartwheel Wrap Completed

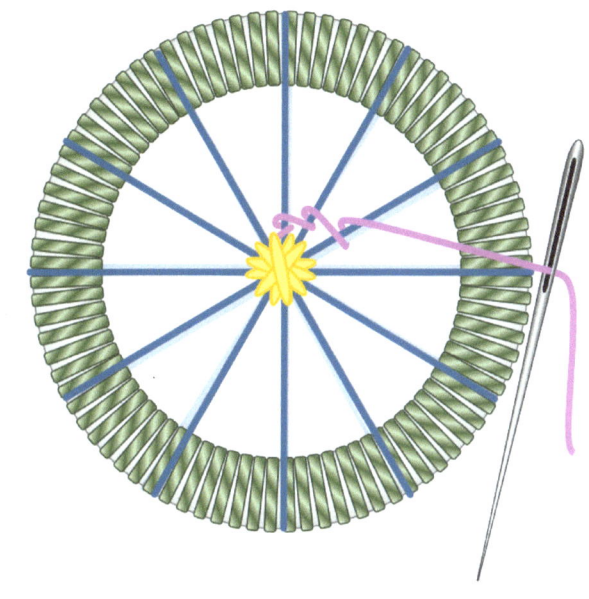

The Second Wrap Completed

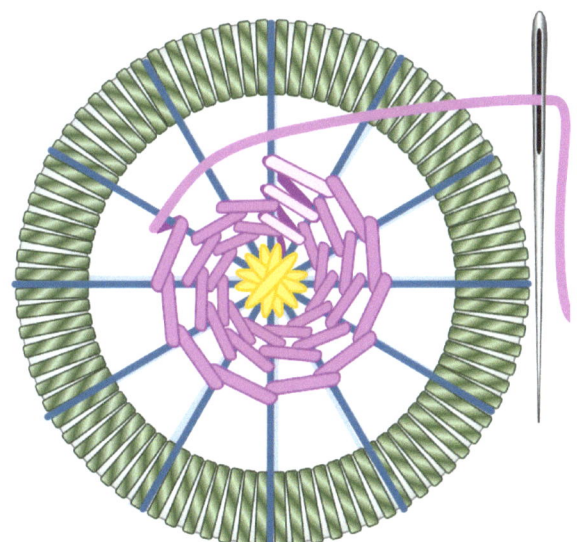

### REVERSE CARTWHEEL WRAP

The spokes are numbered 1-12, with spoke 12 in the "12 o'clock" position. Commence with the threaded needle behind the button, and *working in a clockwise direction, bring the threaded needle up from behind the button and emerge to the left of spoke 12; next, carry the thread over to the right of the next spoke (spoke 1); finally, insert the threaded needle through to the back of the button, and re-emerge to the front of the button up to the left of the spoke that was just covered.

Repeat from * to complete the round, moving over one spoke at a time in a clockwise direction, until all of the spokes have been covered with thread.

# *Placing the last wrap of a Reverse Cartwheel Wrap Round*

The first wraps of each *Reverse Cartwheel Wrap* round are shown above in light lavender. The last wrap of each round (shown in orange) needs to nestle in between the first wrap of the current round, and the first wrap of the previous round.

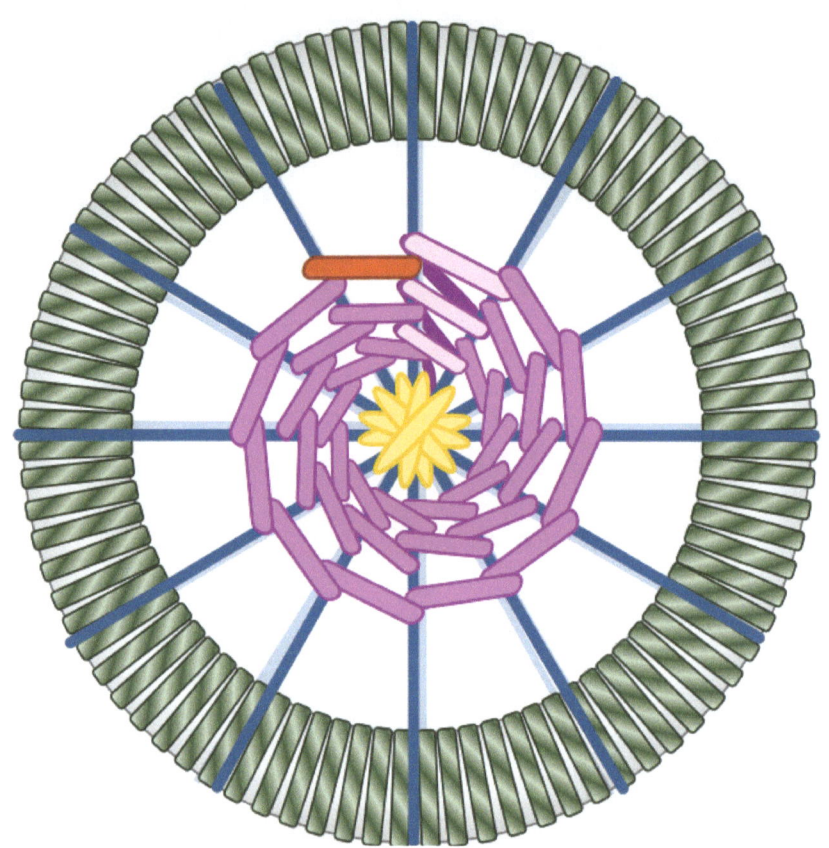

The *Reverse Cartwheel Wrap* adds an exciting dimension to both new and traditional button variations. Some versions of the *Blandford* button make use of this versatile wrap. If you work more than one round in the same (clockwise or counterclockwise) direction, you will achieve a rich ropey texture. If you work a pair of rounds in opposing directions—one round in a clockwise direction, and one round in a counter clockwise direction, the two rounds appear to make a lovely chain.
The illustration above shows a button that has three *Reverse Cartwheel Wrap* rounds, all three of which have been worked in the same (clockwise) direction.

# VARIATION 3: SWANSTON WRAP

Skipping the first spoke of every round and the striking combination of *Single Dorset Cartwheel Wraps* mixed with *Single Dorset Cartwheel Wraps Worked over a Pair of Spokes* gives the traditional Swanston button its characteristic spiral appearance. It only looks complicated: it is genuinely easier to make than it appears. The Swanston button has so much surface interest that it is simply gorgeous when worked in one color of thread.

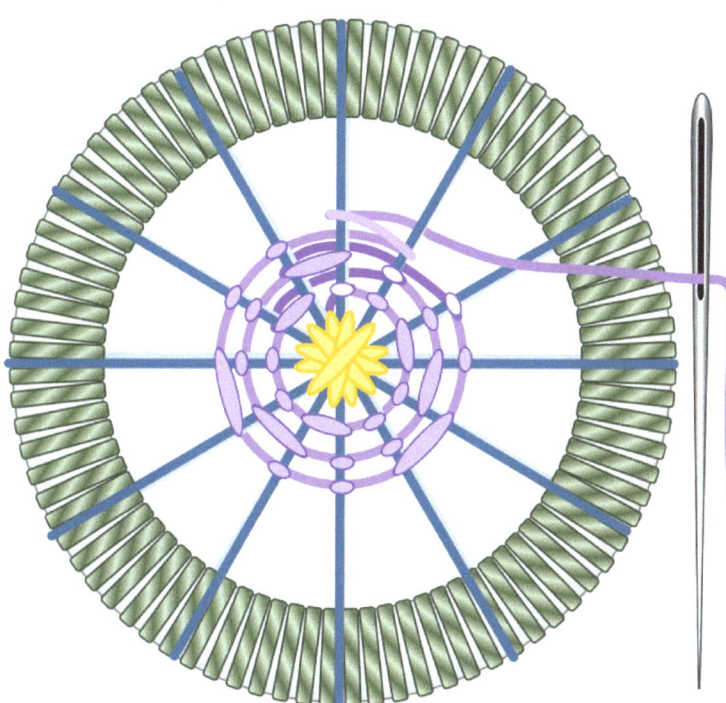

## Swanston Wrap Round

**First round:**
As shown on a 12 spoke button, and proceeding in a clockwise direction *work a *Single Dorset Cartwheel* wrap over each of the next two spokes and then work a *Single Dorset Cartwheel Wrap over a Pair of Spokes* over the next two spokes. Repeat from * 3 more times, to complete the round.

**Second and subsequent rounds:**
Proceeding in a clockwise direction skip the next spoke to begin the next round. *Work a *Single Dorset Cartwheel* wrap over each of the next two spokes and then work a *Single Dorset Cartwheel Wrap over a Pair of Spokes* over the next two spokes. Repeat from * 3 more times, in order to complete the round.

IF YOU ARE GOING TO USE A DIFFERENT SIZE RING, OR A DIFFERENT WEIGHT OF THREAD, WHEN DECIDING HOW MANY SPOKES TO LAY REMEMBER THAT THIS PARTICULAR ITERATION OF THE SWANSTON BUTTON MUST BE WORKED ON A MULTIPLE OF FOUR *LAID SPOKES*.

# Completed Swanston Button

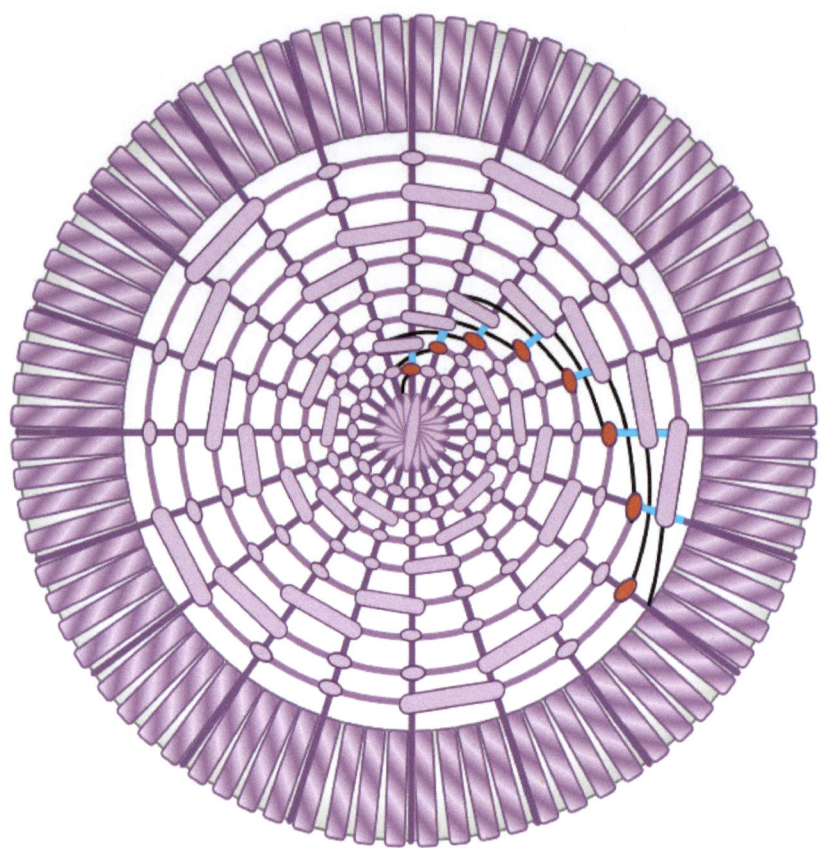

This illustration of a completed Swanston button represents the path that the threaded needle takes, first completing the last wrapped stitch of one round, and then skipping under one spoke, before making the first wrapped stitch of the next round.

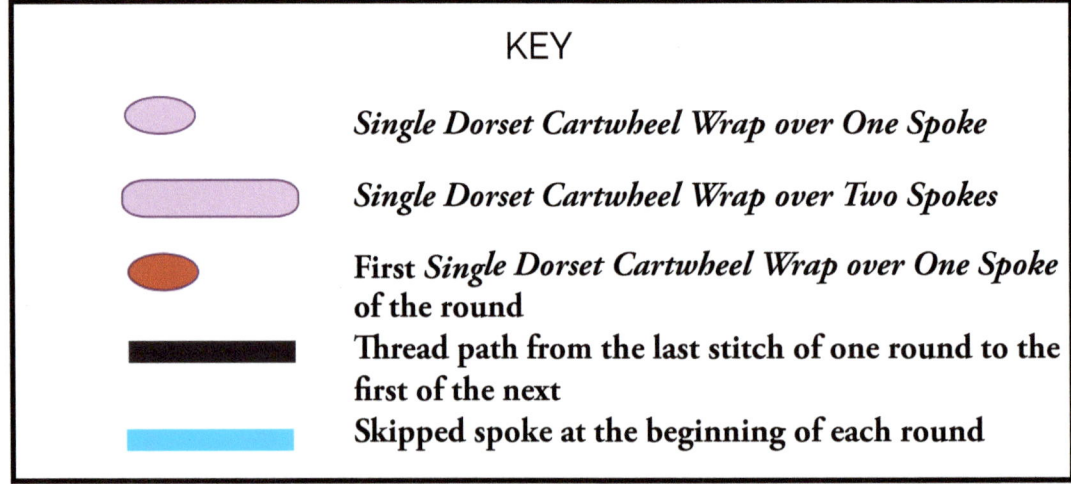

# VARIATION 4: OUTER RING WRAP

## THE FIRST ROUND OF WRAPS IS CROSSED BY THE SECOND ROUND OF WRAPS WHICH ARE WORKED IN THE OPPOSITE DIRECTION.

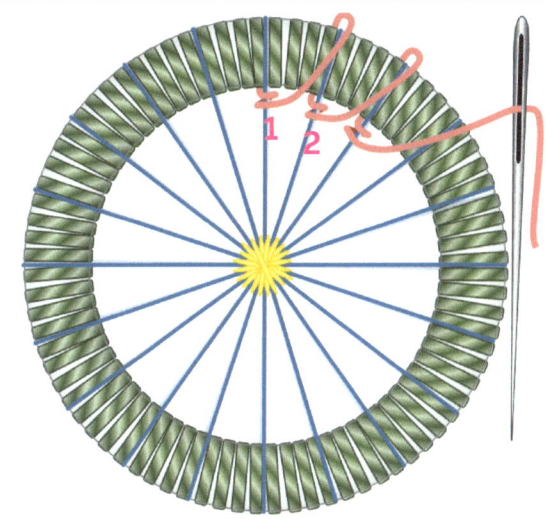

This is a 20 spoke button. The spokes are numbered 1-20 with spoke 1 in the "12 o'clock position.

## Outer Ring Wrap
### clockwise direction

1 Work close to the ring. Bring the threaded needle up to the front of the button, in the space to the left of spoke 1; next, insert the needle down through the space to the right of spoke 1; finally, bring the threaded needle to the front, emerging in the space to the left of spoke 1—first spoke encircled with thread.

2. Travel to the next spoke by carrying the threaded needle up and over the ring to the right of the spoke (2), nestling this thread in between the spoke and a cast knot on the ring, keeping a finger on it to hold it in place. Bring the threaded needle to the front of the button, emerging in the space to the left of the spoke (2); next, insert the needle down into the space to the right of the spoke (2); finally, bring the threaded needle back up to the front, emerging in the space to the left of the spoke (2)—second spoke encircled with thread. Repeat step 2 until you have encircled each spoke with thread. Secure and clip the thread, behind the first spoke that you covered.

## Outer Ring Wrap
### counter clockwise direction

(Shown below worked over 1 round of Outer Ring Wraps worked in a clockwise direction)

1. Work close to the previous round. Bring the threaded needle up to the front of the button, in the space to the right of spoke 1; next, insert the needle down through the space to the left of spoke 1; finally, bring the threaded needle back up to the front, emerging in the space to the right of spoke 1—first spoke encircled with thread.

2. Travel to the next spoke by carrying the threaded needle up and over the ring to the left of the spoke (20). Bring the threaded needle to the front of the button emerging in the space to the right of the spoke (20); next, insert the needle down into the space to the left of the spoke (20); finally, bring the threaded needle back up to the front, emerging in the space to the right of the spoke (20)—second spoke encircled with thread. Repeat step 2 until you have encircled each spoke with thread. Secure and clip the thread behind the first spoke that you covered.

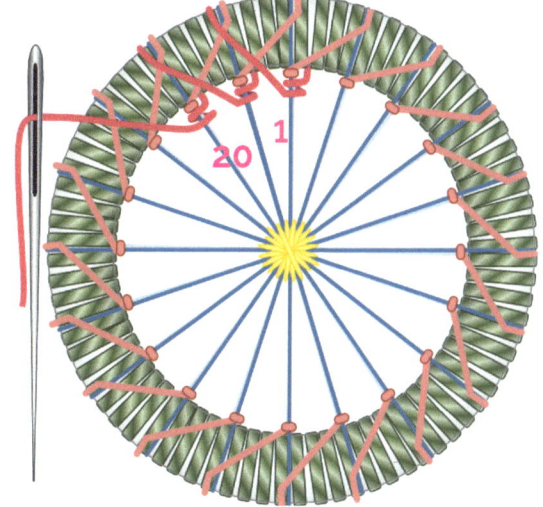

# CONSTRUCTING THE JEWELRY

### Sew Two Rings (or Buttons) Together

(Illustration at right)
Using the chenille needle, sew one ring (or button) to another ring or button by stitching them together through their adjoining *Cast Knots*. You may use the excess threads that are already attached to the buttons to sew them together, or you may attach a new piece of thread. Secure and clip the thread.

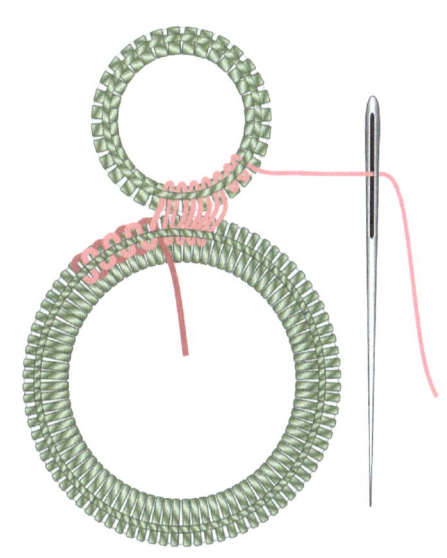

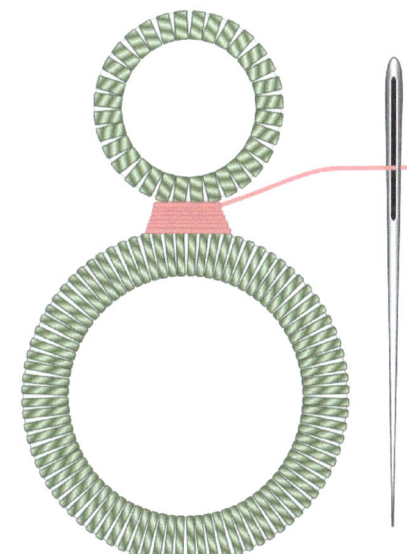

### Cover the juncture with thread

(Illustration at left)
Preparation: Thread the chenille needle and attach the thread to the underside of the ring securely, then neatly wrap the juncture of the rings or the buttons (the spot where the two touch) with thread until it is fully covered. Secure in an unobtrusive place underneath the buttons and clip the thread.

# CORD AND CLOSURES

Cord can be made out of any weight of almost any fiber—wool, cotton, silk, linen, rayon, and most synthetics. All of the cords in this book were made from DMC *Cébélia Crochet Thread size 10*. Crochet thread is ideal, as it is a nice weight, it is smooth and strong, and the balls have a lot of yardage. It is important to be very generous when cutting lengths of thread to make cord. Almost all of the projects in this book were made using 4 strands of thread, which when doubled up yields an 8 strand cord. If you use more strands of thread, you will make a wider cord.

You will need to cut strands of thread at least 2 times your desired finished length plus at least 12-18 inches/ 31-46 cm to allow for knotting the ends. You may cut the finished cord to any length you need, but plan ahead for extra length so that you can knot the thread at the cut end so it doesn't unwind, and remember that you will need enough cord to knot your jewelry to keep it closed.

To make the cord: Make a neat bundle of the cut strands, matching the ends evenly. Fold the bundle of threads in half, and place the fold of the threads (the halfway point) around a stable base, such as a sturdy table leg, a hook or a knob. Knot the cut ends together, and then, gripping the knot in your hand, step away from the base until the length of thread is almost taut. Twist the threads in a clockwise or counterclockwise direction—it doesn't matter as long as you are consistent—until the thread starts to double up on itself. I like to keep twisting for a little longer until the thread becomes almost impossibly taut and really begins to kink up. Fold the entire twisted length of thread in half and let the two bundles of thread wind up against each other until the whole length of cord is twisted together. Cut the thread carefully from the base, and knot the ends together so it doesn't untwist. Smooth the length of cord, spreading the twists evenly.

### Approximate Finished Cord Lengths

All of these measurements are for a cord made from 4 strands of #10 cotton crochet thread. Different fiber, tension, or number of strands, as well as the size of the stable base you wrap your threads around, will change the size of your finished cord.

| Thread Length | Strands of Thread | Finished Cord |
|---|---|---|
| 36 inches/91 cm | 4 | ~11 inches/ 28 cm |
| 45 inches/114 cm | 4 | ~16 inches/ 41 cm |
| 60 inches/152 cm | 4 | ~22 inches/ 56 cm |
| 72 inches/183 cm | 4 | ~27 inches/ 69 cm |
| 84 inches/213 cm | 4 | ~33 inches/ 84 cm |
| 96 inches/244 cm | 4 | ~37 inches/ 94 cm |
| 120 inches/305 cm | 4 | ~48 inches/ 122 cm |

## Larks Head Knot

  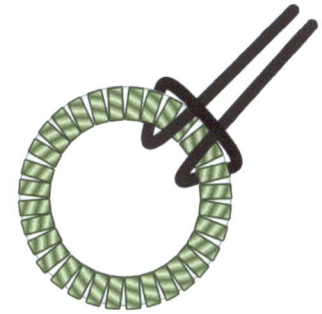

**Step 1**
Fold the twisted cord in half and place it flat on your workspace, then place the ring on top of the cord.

**Step 2**
Pick up the two cut ends of the twisted cord, and bring them up and over the ring, and then through the folded loop.

**Step 3**
Pull evenly on the cord ends until the knot is snug up against the ring, making sure that the cord ends are the same length.

## Closures

There are many ways to finish a cord necklace, anklet, or bracelet. You can attach a metal toggle, lobster, box, or magnetic clasp to the finished cord, or you can just knot the raw edges together. My favorite is a knotted slider clasp, and I think it is an elegant and useful closure. The *Cast Knots* encase the crossed cords.

## Knotted Slider Clasp

**Step 1 (bottom left):** Cross the two knotted ends of the jewelry cord, one over the other.

**Step 2 (bottom center):** Thread a tapestry needle with 2 18 inch/46cm pieces of the cord thread. Make about 6-10 firm, but not tight, *Cast Knots* over the junction of both of the cords. Be careful not to catch any of the cord as the cord ends need to be able to slide through the clasp. Secure and clip the thread cautiously so that you don't catch any of the cord in your stitches.

**Step 3 (bottom right):** Make a stopper knot (a simple over hand knot) in the cord a small distance from each side of the clasp. The stopper knots will make your knotted clasp slightly adjustable, and will help keep the cord from opening up, or from closing too tightly.

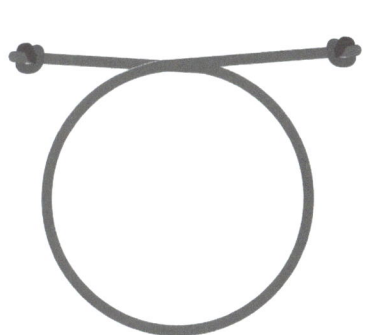 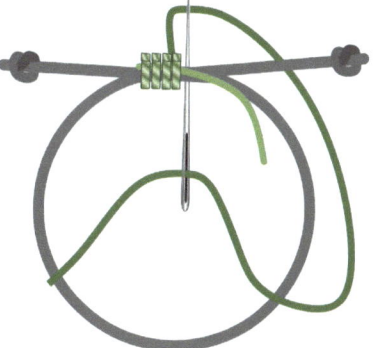 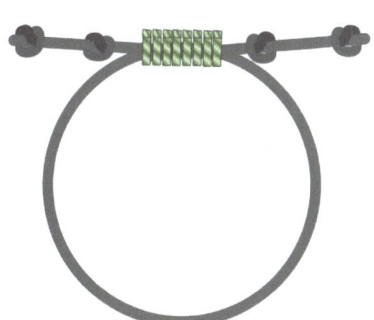

THE PATTERNS

**Dorset Cartwheel button**
(pictured above) with 84 *Cast Knots*, 12 *Laid spokes* and 7 rounds of *Single Dorset Cartwheel Wraps Over One Spoke.*

# DORSET CARTWHEEL JEWELRY

The **Dorset Cartwheel button** is the very first button that every novice button maker should try to make. Not only is it the quintessential thread wrapped button, but more significantly, making one will teach you all of the steps that you will need to know. The basic *Casting, Slicking, Laying, and Rounding* steps, can be applied to create almost every variation of button that you can imagine.

# PROJECT № 1 DORSET CARTWHEEL EARRINGS

TIMELESSLY BEAUTIFUL, THIS HERITAGE BUTTON HAS BEEN IN VOGUE FOR NEARLY THREE HUNDRED YEARS

## Materials

Each project requires a ruler or a tape measure and a small sharp pair of scissors.

**Thread**
- 1 skein DMC *Article #115 Pearl Cotton Size 5* in color A #340 Blue Violet-medium

**Rings**
- 2 plastic or coated metal rings, each with an outer diameter of 1 inch/2.5 cm

**Jewelry Findings**
- One pair of metal earring hooks in silver

**Needles**
- Tapestry needle size 16
- Chenille needle size 18 or 20

## Dorset Button Earrings

### Dorset Buttons (Make 2)

**Preparation** Thread the tapestry needle with 3 ½ yards/3.1 m of color C thread.

**Step 1–Casting**
Make 84 Cast Knots to cover the ring.

**Step 2—Slicking**
Gently nudge the knots at the outer edge of the ring to the underside of the ring.

**Step 3A—Laying**
Lay 12 equidistant spokes. The ring shown has 12 spokes with 7 Cast Knots in between each spoke. Make sure that each spoke has a bottom and a top thread.

**Step 3B—Anchoring**
Anchor and center all of the spokes in the middle with a few straight stitches (forming a "+" and then an "x", and repeating as necessary, in a clockwise fashion) to secure and align the spokes. It is very important to anchor the spokes as close to the center of the button as possible, or your finished button will not be even.

**Step 4— Rounding**
Fill in the spokes with rounds of *Single Dorset Cartwheel Wraps* until the spokes are completely covered. Secure the thread on the underside of the button. Do not cut the excess thread, as you may want to use it later to sew on the earring hook.

### Attach the earring hook

Thread the chenille needle with 12 inches /30.5cm of thread and then attach the thread to the underside of the button at the top of the ring, or use the thread end left from the previous step to sew the earring hook to the button. Center the earring hook and sew it firmly to the top of the button. Secure and clip the thread.

**Finishing**
Secure any loose threads and clip the ends.

**Finished Measurement:** 1 inch/2.5 cm drop (not including earring hook)

MATERIALS: Each project requires a ruler or a tape measure and a small sharp pair of scissors.

**Threads**

*Pink Earrings (shown on page 39)*
- 1 skein DMC *Article #115 Pearl Cotton Size 5* in each of color A #818 Baby Pink, color B #776 Pink-medium, and color C #760 Salmon
- 1 spool DMC *Diamant Grandé* in color D #G225 Old Rose

*Blue Earrings*
- 1 skein DMC *Article #115 Pearl Cotton Size 5* in each of color A #828 Blue-ultra very light, color B #827 Blue-very light, and color C #824 Blue–very dark
- 1 spool DMC *Diamant Grandé* in color D #G415 Dark Silver

**Rings** For one pair of earrings:
- 4 plastic or coated metal rings each with an outer diameter of ½ inch/1.25 cm
- 2 plastic or coated metal rings each with an outer diameter of ¾ inch/1.9 cm

**Jewelry Findings**
- For the Pink Earrings: one pair of metal earring hooks in gold
- For the Blue Earrings: one pair of metal earring hooks in silver

**Needles**
- Tapestry needle size 16
- Chenille needle size 18 or 20

# PROJECT № 2  TRIPLE DANGLE EARRINGS

TIERED CAST RINGS AND METALLIC ACCENTS LEND THESE
BREEZY EARRINGS A "WEAR WITH EVERYTHING" AIR

## Triple Dangle Earrings

### Cast rings
(Make 4—2 in color A and 2 in color B)

**Preparation:** Thread the tapestry needle with 1 yard/.9m of thread.

**Step 1—Casting**
Make 36 Cast Knots to cover the ring.

**Step 2—Slicking**
Gently nudge the knots at the outer edge of the ring to the underside of the ring.

**Finishing**
Secure the thread on the underside of the button. Remove the needle. Do not cut the excess thread, as you may wish to use it to sew this ring to another ring.

### Dorset buttons (Make 2)
**Preparation**
Thread the tapestry needle with 2 yards/1.8m of color C thread.

**Step 1—Casting**
Make 50 Cast Knots to cover the ring.

**Step 2—Slicking**
Gently nudge the knots at the outer edge of the ring to the underside of the ring..

**Step 3A—Laying**
Lay 10 equidistant spokes. The ring shown has 10 spokes with 5 Cast Knots in between each spoke. Make sure that each spoke has a bottom and a top thread.

**Step 3B—Anchoring**
Anchor and center the spokes in the middle with a few straight stitches (forming a "+" and then an "x", repeating as necessary in a clockwise fashion) to secure and align.

**Step 4—Rounding**
Fill in the spokes with 5 rounds of *Single Dorset Cartwheel Wraps*.

**Finishing**
Secure the thread on the underside of the button. Remove the needle. Do not cut the excess thread, as you may wish to use it to attach this ring to another ring.

### Earring Assembly
**Step 1— Sew the button and rings together**
Using the chenille needle, sew the rings together in this order: Cast ring A to Cast ring B, then Cast ring B to Dorset button C, by stitching them together through their adjoining Cast Knots. You may use the threads that are attached to the buttons, or you may attach a new piece of thread. Secure and clip the threads.

**Step 2—Cover the junctures with thread**
Thread the chenille needle with 1 yard/.9m of color D thread. Attach the thread under the ring and wrap the juncture of two rings (the spot where you attached two rings, or a ring and a button together) with thread until it is fully covered. Secure and clip the thread. Repeat this for all remaining junctures.

**Step 3—Attach the earring hook**
Thread the chenille needle with 12 inches /30.5cm of color D thread. Attach the thread under the top of the color A Cast ring, center the earring hook and sew it firmly to the top of the ring. Secure and clip the thread.

**Finished Measurement:** 1¾ inch/4.5cm drop (not including earring hook)

# PROJECT № 3  DORSET FRINGE EARRINGS

## ADD A FLIRTY TASSEL TO GO FROM DAINTY TO DAZZLING

### MATERIALS
Each project requires a ruler or a tape measure and a small sharp pair of scissors.

**Thread**
- 1 skein DMC *Article #115 Pearl Cotton Size 5* in color A #792 Cornflower Blue-dark

**Rings**
- 2 plastic or coated metal rings, each with an outer diameter of ¾ inch/2 cm

**Jewelry Findings**
- One pair of metal earring hooks in silver

**Needles**
- Tapestry needle size 16
- Chenille needle size 18 or 20

### DORSET BUTTON EARRINGS

**Dorset Buttons** (Make 2)

**Preparation** Thread the tapestry needle with 2 yards/1.8 m of color A thread.

**Step 1–Casting**
Make 60 Cast Knots to cover the ring.

**Step 2—Slicking**
Gently nudge the knots at the outer edge of the ring to the underside of the ring.

**Step 3A—Laying**
Lay 12 equidistant spokes. The ring shown has 12 spokes with 5 Cast Knots in between each spoke. Make sure that each spoke has a bottom and a top thread.

**Step 3B—Anchoring**
Anchor and center all of the spokes in the middle of the button with a few straight stitches (forming a "+" and then an "x", and repeating as necessary, in a clockwise fashion) to secure and align the spokes.

**Step 4— Rounding**
Fill in the spokes with rounds of *Single Dorset Cartwheel Wraps* until the spokes are completely covered. Secure the thread on the underside of the button. Do not cut the excess thread, as you may want to use it to sew on the hook.

**Earring Assembly**
Thread the chenille needle with 12 inches /30.5cm of thread or use the excess thread from step 3. Center the earring hook and sew it firmly to the top of the ring. Secure and clip the thread.

**Make the Fringe**
Cut a 12 inch/30.5 cm piece of thread. Put it aside. Cut 35 6 inch/15cm lengths of thread. Stack the cut threads neatly into a bundle. Center the 12 inch/30.5cm piece of thread across the bundle of cut threads, and then fold the bundle of threads neatly in half over the single piece of thread and use the thread to tie the bundle of cut threads at the fold together firmly— fringe made.

**Cinch the top of the fringe**
Cut a ½ yard/.45m of thread, and starting about ¼ inch/.6 cm from the tied end of the folded fringe, wind the thread 10 times around the fringe to encircle all of the threads. Secure and clip the thread ends.

**Sew the fringe to the bottom of the button**
Thread the chenille needle with color A thread and sew the fringe to the button. Trim the bottom of the fringe evenly with sharp scissors.

**Cover the juncture with thread**
Thread the chenille needle with 18 inches/46 cm of thread. Attach the thread underneath the ring and wrap the spot where the button and the fringe are attached with thread 8 times. Secure and clip the threads.

**Finished Measurement:** 1 inch/2.5 cm drop (not including earring hook)

# PROJECT № 4 DORSET CARTWHEEL WITH CAST RING EARRINGS

## THE PRECIOUS METAL GLEAM AT THE JUNCTURE OF THE RINGS UNDERSCORES THE OPULENCE OF THESE EARRINGS

### MATERIALS

Each project requires a ruler or a tape measure and a small sharp pair of scissors.

### Threads

#### Green and Teal Earrings

This colorway uses 1 skein of DMC *Article #115 Color Variations Pearl Cotton Size 5* and 1 skein of DMC *Article #115 Pearl Cotton Size 5* for the rounding step.

- 1 skein DMC *Article #115 Color Variations Pearl Cotton Size 5* in each of color A #4045 Evergreen Forest, and color C #4025 Caribbean Bay
- 1 skein DMC *Article #115 Pearl Cotton Size 5* in color B #991 Aquamarine-dark
- 1 spool DMC *Diamant Grandé* in color D #G3821 Light Gold

#### Blue and Purple Earrings

This colorway uses 2 skeins of DMC *Article #115 Pearl Cotton Size 5* for the rounding step.

- 1 skein DMC *Article #115 Color Variations Pearl Cotton Size 5* in color A #4240 Midsummer Night
- 1 skein DMC *Article #115 Pearl Cotton Size 5* in each of color B #553 Violet, and color C #554 Violet-light
- 1 spool DMC *Diamant Grandé* in color D #G415 Dark Silver

#### Yellow and Peach Earrings

This colorway uses 2 skeins of DMC Pearl Cotton Size 5 for the rounding step.

- 1 skein DMC *Article #115 Color Variations Pearl Cotton Size 5* in color A #4090 Golden Oasis
- 1 skein DMC *Article #115 Pearl Cotton Size 5* in each of color B #353 Peach, and color C #819 Baby Pink-light
- 1 spool DMC *Diamant Grandé* in color D #G225 Old Rose

### Rings For one pair of earrings:

- 2 plastic or coated metal rings each with an outer diameter of ½ inch/1.25 cm
- 2 plastic or coated metal rings each with an outer diameter of 1 inch/2.5 cm

### Jewelry Findings

- For the *Green and Teal*, or the *Yellow and Peach Earrings*: one pair of metal earring hooks in gold
- For the *Blue and Purple* earrings: one pair of metal earring hooks in gold

### Needles

- Tapestry needle size 16
- Chenille needle size 18 or 20

**Finished Measurement:** 1½ inch/3.75cm drop (not including earring hook)

# Dorset Cartwheel with Cast ring Earrings

**Cast rings** (make 2 in color A)
**Preparation** Thread the tapestry needle with 1 yard/.9m of color A thread.
**Step 1—Casting**
Make 36 Cast Knots to cover a ½ inch/1.25cm ring.
**Step 2—Slicking**
Gently nudge the knots at the outer edge of the ring to the underside of the ring.
**Finishing**
Secure the thread on the underside of the button. Remove the needle. Do not cut the excess thread, as you may wish to use it to attach this ring to the button ring.

**Dorset buttons** (Make 2)
**Preparation** Thread the tapestry needle with 2 yards/1.8m of color A thread.
**Step 1—Casting**
Make 84 Cast Knots to cover a 1 inch/2.5 cm ring.
**Step 2—Slicking**
Gently nudge the knots at the outer edge of the ring to the underside of the ring.
**Step 3A—Laying**
Lay 12 equidistant spokes. The ring shown has 12 spokes with 7 Cast Knots in between each spoke. Make sure that each spoke has a bottom and a top thread. Anchor and center the spokes in the middle with a few straight stitches (forming a "+" and then an "x", repeating as necessary in a clockwise fashion) to secure and align.

### Step 4—Rounding
Thread a chenille needle with 1 yard/.9m of color B thread. Attach the thread underneath the button.
### Rounds 1-3
Work 3 rounds of *Single Dorset Cartwheel Wraps*. Secure and clip the thread.
Switch colors by threading a chenille needle with 1 yard/.9m of color C thread. Attach the thread to the underside of the button.
### Rounds 4-6
Work 3 rounds of *Single Dorset Cartwheel Wraps*. Secure and clip the thread.
Switch colors by threading a chenille needle with 1 yard/.9m of color D thread. Attach the thread to the underside of the button.
### Round 7
Work 1 round of *Reverse Cartwheel Wraps*. Secure and clip the thread.

## Earring Assembly
### Step 1—Sew the button and ring together
Using the chenille needle, sew one Cast ring to one Dorset button by stitching them together through their adjoining Cast Knots. You may use the threads that are attached to sew them together, or you may attach a new piece of thread. Secure and clip the thread.
### Step 2—Cover the juncture with thread
Thread the chenille needle with 1 yard/.9m of color D thread. Attach the thread to the underside of the ring and wrap the juncture (the spot where you attached the button and the ring together) with thread until it is fully covered. Secure and clip the thread.
### Step 3—Attach the earring hook
Thread the chenille needle with 12 inches/30.5cm of color D thread. Attach the thread under the ring at the top of the Cast ring, center the earring hook and sew it firmly to the top of the ring. Secure and clip the thread.

# PROJECT № 5 DORSET CARTWHEEL BROOCH

THIS STATEMENT PIN SHOWCASES YOUR FAVORITE OVER-DYED THREAD

## MATERIALS

Each project requires a ruler or a tape measure and a small sharp pair of scissors.

**Threads**

- 1 skein DMC *Article #115 Color Variations Pearl Cotton Size 5* in color A #4240 Midsummer Night
- 1 skein DMC *Article #115 Pearl Cotton Size 5* in each of colors B #553 Violet, C #340 Blue Violet-medium, and color D #792 Cornflower Blue- dark

**Rings**

- 1 plastic or coated metal ring with an outer diameter of 1½ inches /3.75 cm

**Jewelry Findings**

- One pin back

**Needles**

- Tapestry needle size 16
- Chenille needle size 18 or 20

## DORSET BUTTON BROOCH

### Dorset Button

**Preparation** Thread the tapestry needle with 3 ½ yds/ 3.2 m of color A thread.

**Step 1—Casting**

Make 120 Cast Knots to cover the ring.

**Step 2—Slicking**

Gently nudge the knots at the outer edge of the ring to the underside of the ring.

Switch colors by threading a chenille needle with 3½ yards/3.2m of color B thread. Attach the thread to the underside of the ring.

**Step 3A—Laying**

Lay 12 equidistant spokes. The ring shown has 12 spokes with 10 Cast Knots in between each spoke. Make sure that each spoke has a bottom and a top thread.

**Step 3B—Anchoring**

Anchor and center the spokes in the middle with a few straight stitches (forming a "+" and then an "x", repeating as necessary in a clockwise fashion) to secure and align.

**Step 4—Rounding**

1. Fill in the spokes with 8 rounds of *Single Dorset Cartwheel Wraps*. Secure and then clip the thread.

Switch colors by threading a chenille needle with 2 yards/1.8m of color C thread. Attach the thread to the underside of the button.

2. Fill in the spokes with 3 rounds of *Single Dorset Cartwheel Wraps*. Secure and then clip the thread.

Switch colors by threading a chenille needle with 2 yards/1.8m of color D thread. Attach the thread to the underside of the button

3. Fill in the spokes with 3 rounds of *Single Dorset Cartwheel Wraps*. Secure, but do not cut the excess thread, as you may want to use it to sew on the pin back.

### Assemble the Pin

Thread the chenille needle with 12in/30.5cm of thread or use the thread ends that were left from the previous step. Center the pin back and sew it firmly to the underside of the button. Secure and clip any loose threads.

**Finished Measurement:** 1½ inches/3.75 cm across

**Swanston Button**
The button pictured above has 80 *Cast Knots*, 20 *Laid Spokes*, 1 *Dorset Cartwheel Wrap* round and 7 **Swanston Wrap rounds**

**Swanston Wrap Round** Working in a clockwise direction, skip one spoke, work a *Single Dorset Cartwheel Wrap* over the next spoke, and then work a *Single Dorset Cartwheel Wrap Over a Pair of Spokes* (one wrap which encircles the following two spokes at the same time). *Work a Single Dorset Cartwheel Wrap* over each of the next two spokes then work a *Single Dorset Cartwheel Wrap Over a Pair of Spokes*. Repeat from * 4 more times, to complete the round. Skipping the first spoke at the beginning of each round is what gives the **Swanston button** its characteristic spiral.

# SWANSTON BUTTON JEWELRY

The **Swanston button** is deceptive: it looks complicated, but is actually simple to make and it is one of the most beloved of the traditional Dorset button variations. The **Swanston**, with its beguiling spiral center, enhances both classic and trendy ensembles equally beautifully.

# PROJECT № 6  SWANSTON BUTTON EARRINGS

## AN INTRIGUING SPIRAL IMPARTS A CONTEMPORARY FLAIR

## Materials
Each project requires a ruler or a tape measure and a small sharp pair of scissors.

**Thread**
- 1 skein DMC *Article #115 Pearl Cotton Size 5* in color A #340 Blue Violet-medium

**Rings**
- 2 plastic or coated metal rings, each with an outer diameter of 1 inch /2.5 cm

**Jewelry Findings**
- One pair of metal earring hooks in silver

**Needles**
- Tapestry needle size 16
- Chenille needle size 18 or 20

## Swanston Button Earrings

**Swanston Button** (Make 2)

**Preparation** Thread the tapestry needle with a 3 yard/2.7m piece of thread.

**Step 1—Casting**
Make 80 Cast Knots to cover the ring.

**Step 2—Slicking**
Gently nudge the knots at the outer edge of the ring to the underside of the ring.

**Step 3A—Laying**
Lay 20 equidistant spokes. The ring shown has 20 spokes with 4 Cast Knots in between each spoke. The spokes will be referred to as spokes 1-20, with spoke 1 in the "12 o'clock" position. Make sure each spoke has a bottom and a top thread.

**Step 3B—Anchoring**
Anchor and center the spokes in the middle with a few straight stitches (forming a "+" and then an "x", repeating as necessary in a clockwise fashion) to secure and align. It is very important to anchor the spokes as close to the center of the button as possible, or your finished button will not be even.

**Step 4—Rounding**
**Round 1**
Commencing at spoke 1, work 1 round of *Single Dorset Cartwheel Wraps*.

**Rounds 2-8**
Commencing at spoke 1, work 7 rounds of *Swanston Wraps*. Secure the thread on the underside of the button. Remove the needle. Do not cut the excess thread, as you may wish to use it to attach the button to the earring hook.

## Earring Assembly
Thread the chenille needle with a 12 inch/30.5cm piece of thread and attach the thread to the underside of the button at the top of the ring, or use the thread ends left from the previous step to sew the earring hook to the button. Center the earring hook and sew it firmly to the top of the button. Secure and clip the thread.

**Finishing**
Secure any loose threads and clip the ends.

**Finished Measurement:** 1 inch/2.5 cm drop (not including earring hook)

# PROJECT № 7 SWANSTON BUTTON BRACELET

## A GRACEFUL MOTIF POISED ON A TWISTED CORD

### MATERIALS
Each project requires a ruler or a tape measure and a small sharp pair of scissors

**Thread**
- 1 skein DMC *Article #115 Pearl Cotton Size 5* in color A #153 Lilac

**Rings**
- 1 plastic or coated metal ring with an outer diameter of 1 inch /2.5 cm

**Twisted Cord Bracelet**— see pages 40-41
- 2 pieces of twisted cord cut to desired length plus 12 inches/30.5cm to allow for the knotted ends. The cord shown was made using 4 strands of DMC *Cébélia #10 Crochet Thread* in color #310 Black.

**Needles**
- Tapestry needle size 16
- Chenille needle size 18 or 20

### SWANSTON BUTTON BRACELET

**Swanston Button**

**Preparation** Thread the tapestry needle with a 3 yard/ 2.7m piece of thread.

**Step 1—Casting**
Make 80 Cast Knots to cover the ring.

**Step 2—Slicking**
Gently nudge the knots at the outer edge of the ring to the underside of the ring.

**Step 3A—Laying**
Lay 20 equidistant spokes. The ring shown has 20 spokes with 4 Cast Knots in between each spoke. The spokes will be referred to as spokes 1-20, with spoke 1 in the "12 o'clock" position. Make sure each spoke has a bottom and a top thread.

**Step 3B—Anchoring**
Anchor and center the spokes in the middle with a few straight stitches (forming a "+" and then an "x", repeating as necessary in a clockwise fashion) to secure and align.

It is very important to anchor the spokes as close to the center of the button as possible.

**Step 4—Rounding**

**Round 1**
Commencing at spoke 1, work 1 round of *Single Dorset Cartwheel Wraps*.

**Rounds 2-8**
Commencing at spoke 1, work 7 rounds of *Swanston Wraps*. Secure the thread on the underside of the button. Remove the needle. Do not cut the excess thread, as you may wish to use it later to attach the button to the bracelet

### Bracelet Assembly

Knot the two cords together at both ends, to create a double cord bracelet. The bracelet shown has a slider knot closure (see page 41).

Thread the chenille needle with 12 inches /30.5cm of thread and attach the thread to the underside of the button at the top of the ring, or use the thread ends left from the previous step. Center the button and sew it firmly to the top of the bracelet. Secure the thread on the underside of the button and clip the thread.

### Finishing
Secure any loose threads and clip the ends.

**Finished Button Measurement:** 1 inch/2.5cm

# PROJECT № 8 TWO COLOR SWANSTON EARRINGS

A SHIMMER OF SILVER HIGHLIGHTS THE EXQUISITE CURVES OF THIS FAVORITE BUTTON

## MATERIALS

Each project requires a ruler or tape measure and a small sharp pair of scissors.

### Threads
- 1 skein DMC *Article #115 Color Variations Pearl Cotton Size 5* in color A #4022 Mediterranean Sea
- 1 spool DMC *Diamant* in color B #D168 Light Silver

### Rings
- 2 plastic or coated metal rings, each with an outer diameter of 1 inch /2.5 cm

### Jewelry Findings
- One pair of metal earring hooks in silver

### Needles
- Tapestry needle size 16
- Chenille needle size 18 or 20

## Two Color Swanston Button Earrings

**Swanston Button** (Make 2 in color A)

**Preparation** Thread the tapestry needle with a 2 yard/1.8 m piece of color A thread.

**Step 1—Casting**
Make 80 Cast Knots to cover the ring.

**Step 2—Slicking**
Gently nudge the knots at the outer edge of the ring to the underside of the ring.

**Step 3A—Laying**
Lay 20 equidistant spokes. The ring shown has 20 spokes with 4 Cast Knots in between each spoke. The spokes will be referred to as spokes 1-20, with spoke 1 in the "12 o'clock" position. Make sure each spoke has a bottom and a top thread. Secure and clip the thread.

**Step 3B—Anchoring**
Switch colors by threading a chenille needle with 1 yard/.9m of color B thread. Attach the thread to the underside of the center of the spokes. Anchor and center the spokes in the middle with a few straight stitches (forming a "+" and then an "x", repeating as necessary in a clockwise fashion) to secure and align. Secure and clip the thread.

**Step 4—Rounding**
Switch colors by threading a chenille needle with 1½ yards/1.4 m of color A thread. Attach the thread underneath the button.

**Round 1**
Commencing at spoke 1, work 1 round of *Single Dorset Cartwheel Wraps*.

**Rounds 2-6**
Commencing at spoke 1, work 5 rounds of *Swanston Wraps*. Secure and clip the thread.

**Rounds 7-8**
Switch colors by threading a chenille needle with 1 yard/.9m of color B thread. Attach the thread to the underside of the button. Starting at spoke 1, work 2 rounds of *Single Dorset Cartwheel Wraps*. Secure and clip the thread.

## Earring Assembly

Thread the chenille needle with 12 inches /30.5cm of color A thread and attach the thread to the underside of the button at the top of the ring, or use the thread ends left from a previous step to sew the earring hook to the button. Center the earring hook and sew it firmly to the top of the button. Secure and clip the thread.

**Finished Measurement:** 1 inch/2.5 cm drop (not including earring hook)

# PROJECT № 9 CAST RING AND SWANSTON BUTTON NECKLACE

## REFINED GLITTER AND TONAL CAST RINGS FRAME A STUNNING SWANSTON MOTIF

**MATERIALS** Each project requires a ruler or tape measure and a small sharp pair of scissors.

**Threads**
- 1 skein DMC *Article #115 Pearl Cotton Size 5* in each of color A #760 Salmon, color B #761 Salmon-light, and color C #818 Baby Pink
- 1 spool DMC *Diamant Grandé* in color B #G225 Old Rose

**Rings(7)**
- 2 plastic or coated metal rings, each with an outer diameter of ½ inch/1.25 cm
- 2 plastic or coated metal rings, each with an outer diameter of ¾ inch/2 cm
- 2 plastic or coated metal rings, each with an outer diameter of 1 inch/2.5 cm
- 1 plastic or coated metal ring with an outer diameter of 1½ inches/3.75 cm

**Two Part Necklace Cord** — see pages 40-41
- Two cords, each twice the desired length from the Cast ring on the end of the necklace piece, to the back of the neck plus 12 inches/30 cm for knotting the ends. The cord shown was made using 4 strands of DMC *Cébélia #10 Crochet Thread* in color #310 Black.

**Needles**
- Tapestry needle size 16 and a Chenille needle size 18 or 20

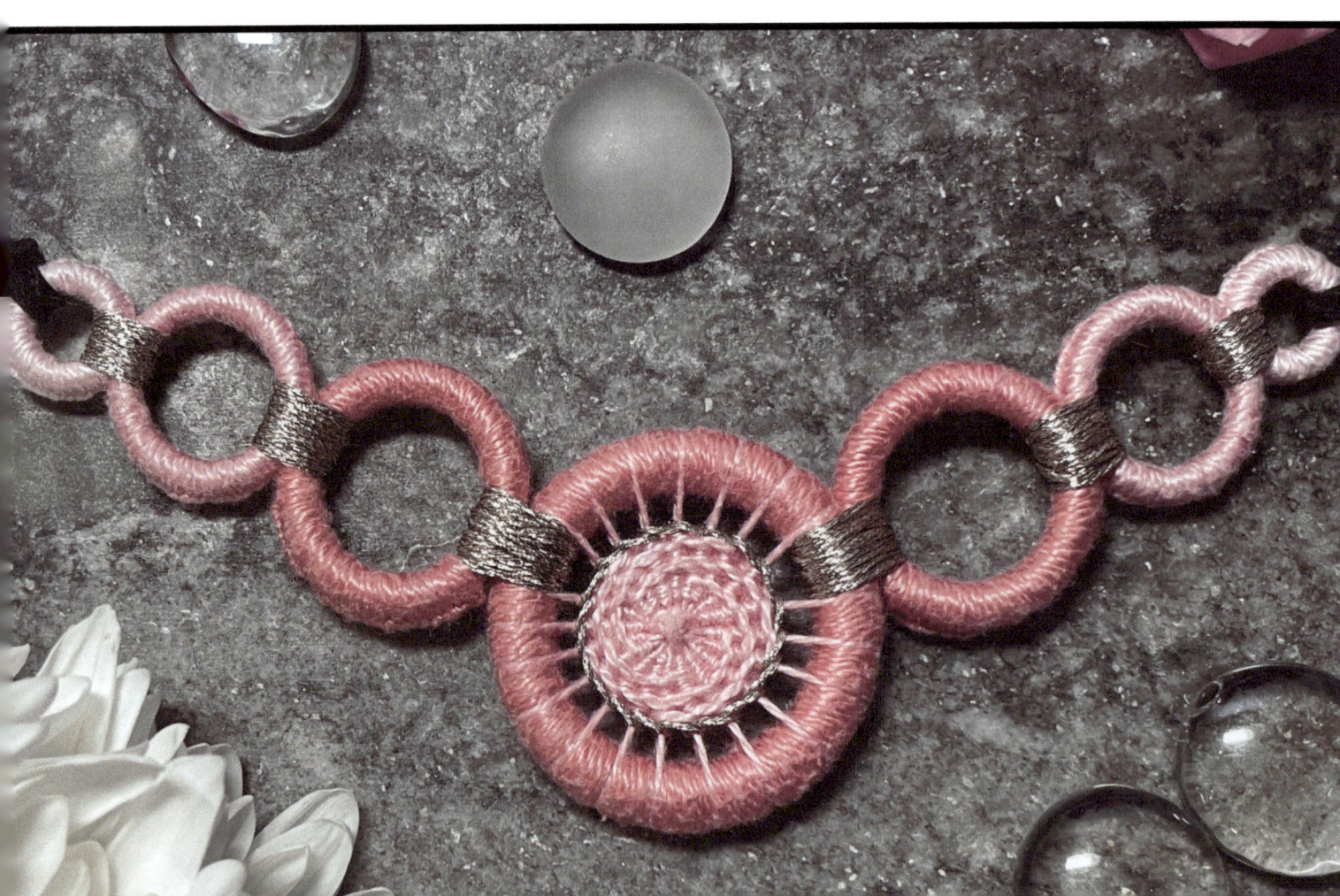

**Finished Necklace Piece Measurement:**
5¾ inches/14.5 cm across

## SWANSTON NECKLACE WITH GRADUATED CAST RINGS

**Swanston Button** (Make 1)
**Preparation** Thread the tapestry needle with a 3 yard/2.7 m piece of color A thread.
**Step 1—Casting**
Make 120 Cast Knots to cover the 1½ inch/3.75 cm ring.
**Step 2—Slicking**
Gently nudge the knots at the outer edge of the ring to the underside of the ring.
Secure and clip the thread.
**Step 3A—Laying**
Thread the chenille needle with a 3½ yard/3.2m piece of color B thread and attach the thread to the underside of the ring. Lay 20 equidistant spokes. The ring shown has 20 spokes with 6 Cast Knots in between each spoke. The spokes will be referred to as spokes 1-20, with spoke 1 in the "12 o'clock" position. Make sure each spoke has a bottom and a top thread.
**Step 3B—Anchoring**
Anchor and center the spokes in the middle with a few straight stitches (forming a "+" and an "x", repeating as necessary in a clockwise fashion) to secure and align.
**Step 4—Rounding**
**Round 1**
Commencing at spoke 1, work 1 round of *Single Dorset Cartwheel Wraps*.
**Rounds 2-10**
Starting at spoke 1, work 9 rounds of *Swanston Wraps*. Secure and clip the thread.
**Round 11**
Switch colors by threading a chenille needle with 1 yard/.9m of color D thread. Attach the thread and starting at spoke 1, work 1 round of *Reverse Cartwheel Wraps*. Secure and clip the thread.

**Cast rings** (Make 6 Cast rings— 2 each of color C (B, A) The directions for each size are in parentheses.

**Preparation** Thread the tapestry needle with 1 yard/.9m (1½ yd/1.3m, 1½ yd/1.3m) of color C (B, A) thread.
**Step 1—Casting**
Make 36 (64, 72) Cast Knots to cover the ring.
**Step 2—Slicking**
Gently nudge the knots at the outer edge of the ring to the underside of the ring. Secure the thread and remove the needle. Do not cut the excess thread, in case you wish to use it to sew on a ring.

## Necklace Assembly
**Step 1—Sew three Cast rings together** (Make 2)
1. Sew one color A Cast ring to one color B Cast ring, and sew one color C Cast ring along the opposite side edge of the color B Cast ring. Refer to the image for placement.
2. Using the chenille needle, sew one of the three Cast ring pieces to each side of the Swanston button by stitching them together through their adjoining Cast Knots. Secure and clip the thread.
**Step 2—Cover all junctures with thread**
Thread the chenille needle with ½ yard/.45 m of color D thread. Attach the thread to the underside of the ring and wrap the juncture (the spot where you attached the button and the ring together) with thread until it is fully covered. Secure and clip the thread.
**Step 3—Attach cord**
Fold one cord in half and make a Lark's head knot to attach it to the Cast ring on the end of the necklace piece. Make a knot very close to the cut ends of the cord, knotting both ends of the cord together. Repeat with the other cord on the Cast ring on the other end of the necklace piece. The necklace shown has a slider knot closure—see page 41.

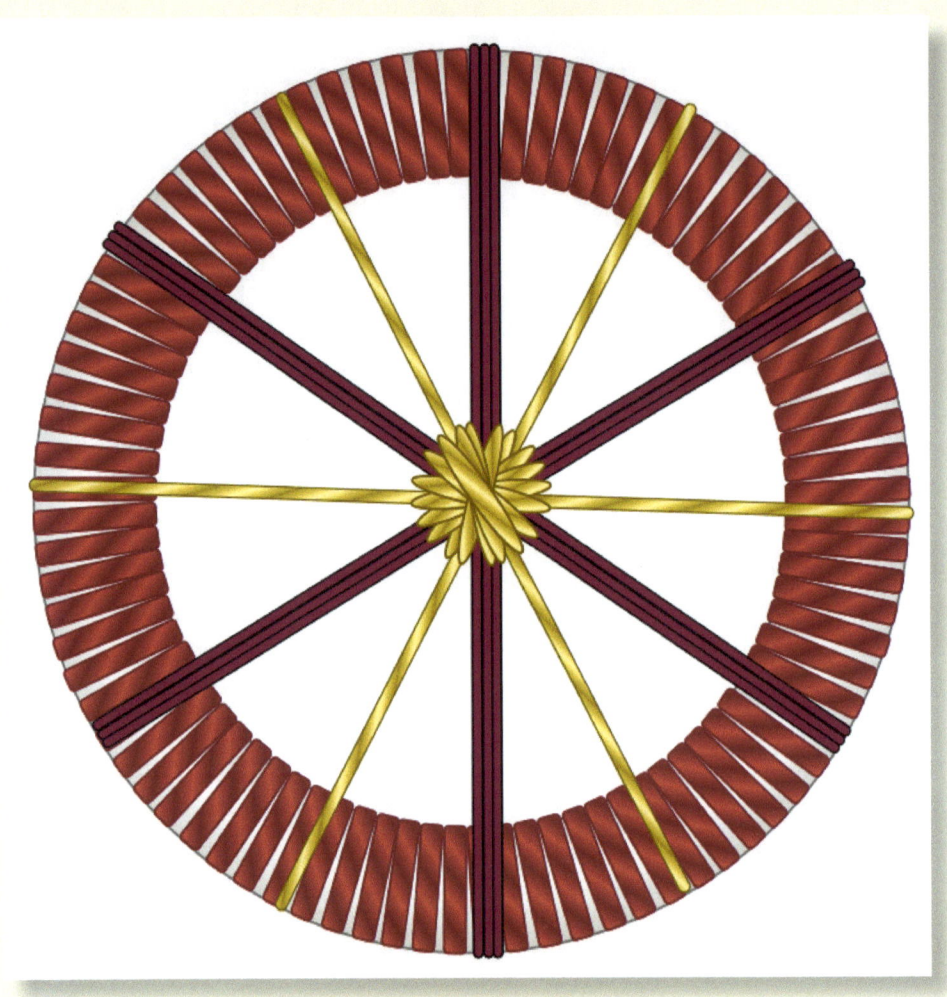

**Simple Spoke Button**
The button pictured above has 84 *Cast Knots*, 6 *Triple Laid* spokes, and 6 *Single Laid* spokes.

# SIMPLE SPOKE JEWELRY

The **Simple Spoke Button** makes use of *Triple Laid* spokes. During the *Laying* step, the thread is wrapped around the diameter of the ring three times (placing all three strands in between two *Cast Knots* as if they were one strand)—one set of *Triple Laid* spokes made. Multiple laid spokes create a ribbon of color which provides a wonderful effect for almost no extra effort.

## MATERIALS
Each project requires a ruler or tape measure and a small sharp pair of scissors.
### Threads
### Red and Gold Earrings (pictured on page 69)
- 1 skein DMC *Article #115 Color Variations Pearl Cotton Size 5* in color A #4210 Radiant Ruby
- 1 skein DMC *Article #115 Pearl Cotton Size 5* in color B #915 Plum-dark
- 1 spool DMC *Diamant Grandé* in color C #G3821 Light Gold

### Pink Earrings
- 1 skein DMC *Article #115 Color Variations Pearl Cotton Size 5* in color A #4190 Ocean Coral
- 1 skein DMC *Article #115 Pearl Cotton Size 5* in each of color B #602 Cranberry-medium, and color C #604 Cranberry-light

### Rings (for one pair of earrings)
- 2 plastic or coated metal rings, each with an outer diameter of ½ inch/1.25 cm
- 2 plastic or coated metal rings, each with an outer diameter of 1 inch/2.5 cm

### Jewelry Findings
- *Red earrings:* pair of gold metal earring hooks, *Pink earrings:* pair of silver metal earring hooks

### Needles
- Tapestry needle size 16 and a Chenille needle size 18 or 20

**Finished Measurement:** 1½ inch/3.75cm drop (not including earring hook)

# PROJECT №10 SIMPLE SPOKE BUTTON DROP EARRINGS

## HARMONIOUS LAID THREAD PAIRINGS GIVE THESE EARRINGS A WORLDLY DEPTH

### Simple Spoke Button Earrings

**Cast rings** (Make 2)

**Preparation** Thread the tapestry needle with 1 yard/.9m of color A thread.

**Step 1—Casting**
Make 36 Cast Knots to cover the ring.

**Step 2—Slicking**
Gently nudge the knots surrounding the ring to the underside of the ring.

**Finishing**
Secure the thread on the underside of the button. Remove the needle. Do not cut the excess thread, as you may wish to use it to attach this ring to another ring.

**Two Color Simple Spoke Button**
(Make 2)

**Preparation:** Thread the tapestry needle with 2 yards/ 1.8m of color A thread.

**Step 1—Casting**
Make 72 Cast Knots to cover a 1 in/2.5 cm ring.

**Step 2—Slicking**
Gently nudge the knots at the outer edge of the ring to the underside of the ring. Secure the thread on the underside of the button. Remove the needle. Do not cut the excess thread, as you may wish to use it to attach this ring to another ring.

**Step 3A—Laying**
Thread a chenille needle with 1 yard/.9m of color B thread. Secure the thread to the underside of the ring.

1. Lay 6 equidistant triple laid spokes (wrap the laying thread completely around the ring three times for each spoke set). The ring shown has 6 triple laid spokes with 12 Cast Knots in between each triple laid spoke. Make sure that each individual spoke has 3 bottom and 3 top threads. Secure and clip the thread.

2. Switch colors by threading a chenille needle with 1 yard/.9m of color C thread. Secure the thread and lay 6 equidistant single laid spokes in between the wraps from step 1. The ring shown has 6 single laid spokes placed 6 Cast Knots apart from each triple laid spoke. Make sure that each individual spoke has a bottom and a top thread.

**Step 3B—Anchoring**
With color C thread, anchor and center the spokes in the middle with straight stitches (forming a "+" and then an "x", repeating as necessary) to align and cover the other threads. Secure and clip the thread.

### Earring Assembly (make 2)

**Step 1—Sew the button to the Cast ring**
Using the chenille needle, sew a Spoke button to a Cast ring by stitching them together through their adjoining Cast Knots. Secure and clip the thread.

**Step 2—Cover the juncture with thread**
Thread the chenille needle with 1 yard/.9m of color C thread. Attach the thread and wrap the juncture of the ring and the button with thread until it is fully covered. Secure and clip the thread.

**Step 3—Attach the earring hook**
Thread the chenille needle with 12 inches /30.5cm of color C thread. Attach the thread underneath the top of the Cast ring, center the earring hook and sew it firmly to the top of the ring. Secure and clip the thread.

# PROJECT № 11 SIMPLE SPOKE PENDANT

THE PURITY OF DESIGN LETS THE SATURATED COLORS TAKE CENTER STAGE

## MATERIALS

Each project requires a ruler or tape measure and a small sharp pair of scissors.

**Threads**
- 1 skein DMC *Article #115 Pearl Cotton Variations Size 5* in color A #4128 Gold Coast
- 1 skein DMC *Article #115 Pearl Cotton Size 5* in colors B #899 Medium Rose
- 1 spool DMC *Diamant* in color C #D301 Copper

**Ring**
- 1 plastic or coated metal ring with an outer diameter of 1½ inches /3.75 cm

**Jewelry Findings**
- One ½ inch/1.25cm silver metal ring

**Twisted Necklace Cord** — see pages 40-41
- One cord the desired length of the necklace piece, plus 12 inches/30 cm for knotting the ends. The cord shown was made using 4 strands of DMC *Cébélia #10 Crochet Thread* in color #310 Black.

**Needles**
- Tapestry needle size 16
- Chenille needle size 18 or 20

## SIMPLE SPOKE PENDANT

### Simple Spoke Button

**Preparation** Thread the tapestry needle with 4 yards/3.9 m of color A thread.

**Step 1—Casting**
Make 120 Cast Knots to cover a 1½ inch /3.75 cm ring

**Step 2—Slicking**
Gently nudge the knots at the outer edge of the ring to the underside of the ring.and then secure the thread on the underside of the ring. Remove the needle. Do not cut the excess thread, as you may wish to use it to attach this ring to another ring.

**Step 3A—Laying**
Thread a chenille needle with 2 yards/1.8 m of color B thread. Secure the thread underneath the ring.

1. Lay 6 equidistant 5 strand laid spokes (wrap the laying thread completely around the ring five times for each spoke set). The ring shown has six 5 strand laid spokes with 10 Cast Knots in between. Make sure that each individual spoke has 5 bottom and 5 top threads. Secure and clip the thread.

2. Thread a chenille needle with a 1 yard/.9m piece of color C thread. Secure the thread to the underside of the ring. Lay 6 equidistant triple laid spokes (wrap the thread 3 times for each spoke) in between the wraps from step 1. The ring shown has 6 triple laid spokes placed 10 Cast Knots apart from each 5 strand laid spoke. Make sure that each individual spoke has 3 bottom and 3 top threads.

**Step 3B—Anchoring**
With color C thread, anchor and center the spokes in the middle with a few stitches (forming a "+" and then an "x", repeating as necessary in a clockwise fashion) to secure and align the center of the spokes. Secure and clip the threads.

### Pendant Assembly

If necessary, attach a new piece of thread. Switch to the chenille needle, center the metal ring (sideways) and sew it firmly to the top of the button. Secure the thread underneath the ring and clip the thread. Thread the necklace cord through the ring. The necklace shown has a slider knot closure—see page 41.

**Finished Button Measurement:** 1½ inches/3.75 cm

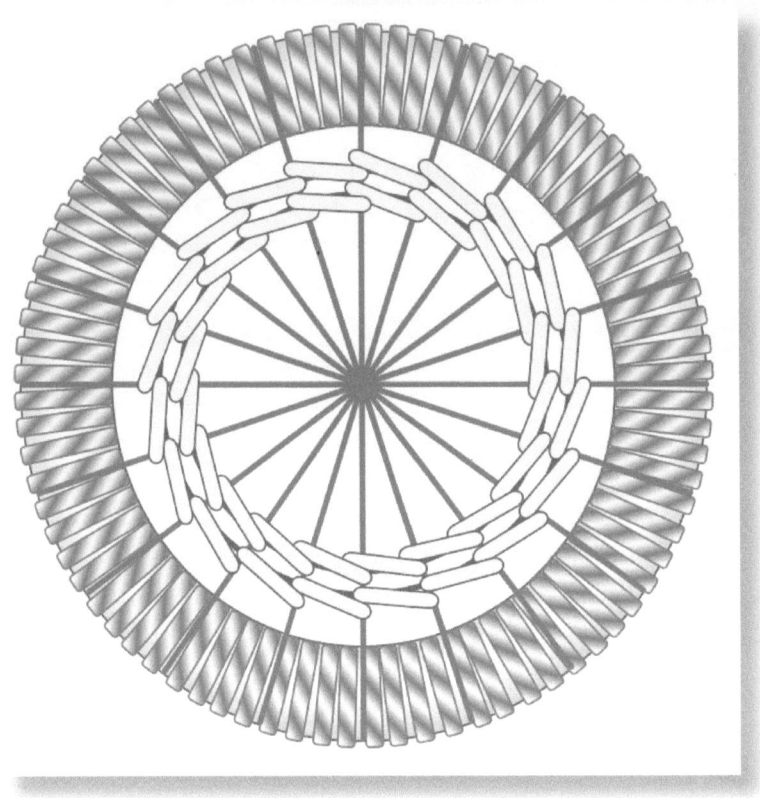
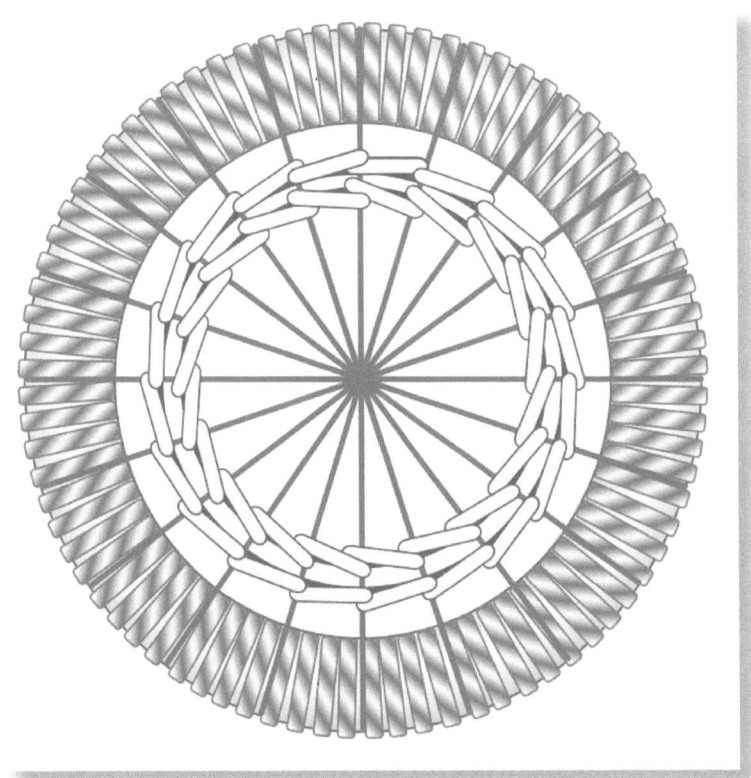

# BLANDFORD BUTTON JEWELRY

The **Blandford buttons** illustrated on the left each have 80 *Cast Knots*, 20 *Laid Spokes* and 2 rounds of *Reverse Cartwheel Wraps*. The top button shows both wrap rounds worked in a clock wise direction. The bottom button shows the two wrap rounds worked in opposite directions, with the first round worked in a clockwise fashion and the second round worked in a counter clockwise fashion, giving a chain like effect. Note that there is no *Anchoring* step for a *Blandford* button.

## Reverse Cartwheel Wrap

*Working in a clockwise direction, bring the threaded needle up from behind the button and emerge to the left of spoke; next, carry the thread over to the right of the next spoke (spoke 2); finally, insert the threaded needle through to the back of the button, and re-emerge to the front of the button up to the left of the spoke just worked. Repeat from * to complete the round.

# PROJECT № 12 BLANDFORD BUTTON EARRINGS

### AN ELEGANT RIFF ON A BELOVED BUTTONY TECHNIQUE

## MATERIALS

Each project requires a ruler or tape measure and a small sharp pair of scissors.

### Threads

#### Red Earrings

- 1 skein DMC *Article #115 Color Variations Pearl Cotton Size 5* in color A #4210 Radiant Ruby
- 1 skein DMC *Article #115 Pearl Cotton Size 5* in color B #814 Garnet-dark

#### Light Blue Earrings (pictured on page 76)

- 1 skein DMC *Article #115 Color Variations Pearl Cotton Size 5* in color A #4020 Tropical Waters

### Rings

- 2 plastic or coated metal rings, each with an outer diameter of 1 inch/2.5 cm

### Jewelry Findings (for each)

- One pair of metal earring hooks in gold

### Needles

- Tapestry needle size 16
- Chenille needle size 18 or 20

## BLANDFORD BUTTON EARRINGS

### Blandford Button (Make 2)

**Preparation**

Thread a tapestry needle with 2 yards/1.8 m of color A thread. Secure the thread to the underside of the ring.

**Step 1—Casting**

Make 80 Cast Knots to cover a 1 in/2.5 cm ring.

**Step 2—Slicking**

Gently nudge the knots at the outer edge of the ring to the underside of the ring..

**Step 3 Laying**

Lay 20 equidistant spokes. The ring shown has 20 laid spokes with 4 Cast Knots in between each laid spoke. The spokes will be referred to as spokes 1-20, with spoke 1 in the "12 o'clock" position. Make sure that each spoke has a bottom and a top thread.

**Step 4—Rounding**

(*For the Red Earrings*)

Switch color thread for this step. Secure and clip the thread behind the button ring, then attach 1 yard/.9m of color B thread.

**Rounds 1-2** (*For the red* and *blue earrings*)

Commencing at spoke 1, work 2 rounds of *Reverse Cartwheel Wraps* in a clockwise direction. Begin the first round very close to the ring, and work the second round next to the first.

### Earring Assembly

If necessary, attach a new piece of thread. Switch to the chenille needle, center the earring hook and sew it firmly to the top of the button. Secure the thread on the underside of the ring and clip the thread.

**Finished Measurement:** 1 inch/2.5 cm drop (not including earring hook)

# PROJECT N⁰ 13 BLANDFORD BUTTON PENDANT

### THE BEAUTIFUL CHAIN EFFECT EDGE IS MADE BY WORKING THE ROUNDING IN TWO DIFFERENT DIRECTIONS

## Materials

Each project requires a ruler or tape measure and a small sharp pair of scissors.

**Thread**
- 1 skein DMC *Article #115 Pearl Cotton Size 5* in color A #794 Cornflower Blue-light

**Ring**
- 1 plastic or coated metal ring with an outer diameter of 1½ inch/3.75 cm

**Jewelry Findings**
- One ½ inch/1.25cm silver metal ring

**Twisted Necklace Cord** — see pages 40-41
- One cord the desired length of the necklace piece, plus 12 inches/30 cm for knotting the ends. The cord shown was made using 4 strands of DMC *Cébélia #10 Crochet Thread* in color #310 Black.

**Needles**
- Tapestry needle size 16
- Chenille needle size 18 or 20

## Blandford Button Pendant

### Blandford Button

**Preparation**

Thread a tapestry needle with 4 yards/3.6 m of color A thread. Secure the thread to the underside of the ring.

**Step 1—Casting**

Make 120 Cast Knots to cover a 1½ inch/3.75cm ring.

**Step 2—Slicking**

Gently nudge the knots at the outer edge of the ring to the underside of the ring.

**Step 3—Laying**

Lay 30 equidistant spokes. The ring shown has 30 laid spokes with 4 Cast Knots in between each laid spoke. The spokes will be referred to as spokes 1-30, with spoke 1 in the "12 o'clock" position. Make sure that each spoke has a bottom and a top thread.

**Step 4—Rounding**

Commencing at spoke 1, work 1 round of *Reverse Cartwheel Wraps* in a clockwise direction. Begin the first round as close as possible to the ring.

**Round 2**

Commencing at spoke 1, work 1 round of *Reverse Cartwheel Wraps* in a counterclockwise direction. Begin the second round as close as possible to the first.

### Pendant Assembly

If necessary, attach a new piece of thread. Switch to the chenille needle, center the metal ring (sideways) and sew it firmly to the top of the button. Secure the thread underneath the ring and clip the thread. Thread the necklace cord through the ring. The necklace shown has a slider knot closure—see page 41.

**Finished Measurement:** 1½ inch /3.75 cm drop (not including ring at top)

## Materials

Each project requires a ruler or tape measure and a small sharp pair of scissors.

### Threads
- 1 skein DMC *Article #115 Pearl Cotton Size 5* in each of colors A #3687 Mauve, and B #3689 Mauve-light
- 1 spool DMC *Diamant Grandé* in color C #G415 Dark Silver

### Rings
- 2 plastic or coated metal rings each with an outer diameter of ¾ inch/1.9 cm

### Jewelry Findings
- One pair of metal earring hooks in silver

### Needles
- Tapestry needle size 16 and a Chenille needle size 18 or 20

# PROJECT №14 BLANDFORD FRINGE EARRINGS

## FRINGE TAKES A HERITAGE BUTTON FROM HUMBLE TO HAUTE COUTURE

### Blandford Button Earrings

**Blandford Button** (Make 2)

**Preparation**
Thread a tapestry needle with 2 yards/1.8m of color A thread. Secure the thread to the underside of the ring.

**Step 1—Casting**
Make 64 Cast Knots to cover a ¾ inch/1.9 cm ring.

**Step 2—Slicking**
Gently nudge the knots at the outer edge of the ring to the underside of the ring.

**Step 3—Laying**
Lay 16 equidistant spokes. The ring shown has 16 laid spokes with 4 Cast Knots in between each laid spoke. Make sure that each spoke has a bottom and a top thread. Secure the thread and remove the needle. Do not cut the excess thread, as you may wish to use it later.

**Step 4—Rounding**
Switch colors by threading a chenille needle with a 1 yard/.9 m piece of color C thread. Secure the thread underneath the ring. Commencing at spoke 1, work 2 rounds of *Reverse Cartwheel Wraps* in a clockwise direction. Begin the first round as close as possible to the ring, and work the second round right next to the first. Secure and clip the thread.

**Finished Measurement:** 1 inch/2.5cm drop (not including earring hook)

**Earring Assembly**
Thread the chenille needle with 12 inches /30.5cm of color A thread or use the excess thread from step 3. Center the earring hook and sew it firmly to the top of the ring. Secure and clip the thread.

**Make the Fringe**
Cut a 12 inch/30.5 cm piece of color B thread. Cut 35 6 inch/15cm lengths of color B thread. Stack the cut threads neatly into a bundle. Center the 12 inch/30.5cm piece of thread across the bundle of cut threads, and then fold the bundle of threads neatly in half over the single piece of thread and use the thread to tie the bundle of cut threads at the fold together firmly— fringe made.

**Cinch the top of the fringe**
Cut an 18 inch/46cm piece of color C thread, and, starting about ¼ inch/.6 cm from the tied end of the folded fringe, wind the thread 10 times around the fringe to encircle all of the threads. Secure and clip the thread ends.

**Sew the fringe to the bottom of the button**
Thread the chenille needle with color A thread and sew the fringe to the button. Trim the bottom of the fringe evenly with sharp scissors.

**Cover the juncture with thread**
Thread the chenille needle with 18 inches/46cm of color C thread. Attach the thread underneath the ring and wrap the spot where the button and the fringe are attached with thread eight times. Secure and clip the threads.

# PROJECT № 15 BLANDFORD BUTTON METALLIC PENDANT

## AN UNEXPECTED SILVER BORDER TRANSFORMS THIS QUINTESSENTIALLY BRITISH BUTTON INTO A TREASURE

**MATERIALS** Each project requires a ruler or tape measure and a small sharp pair of scissors.

**Threads**
- 1 skein DMC *Article #115 Pearl Cotton Size 5* in each of colors A #3687 Mauve, and B #3689 Mauve-light, and C #3685 Mauve-very dark
- 1 spool DMC *Diamant Grandé* in color D #G415 Dark Silver

**Rings**
- 1 plastic or coated metal ring with an outer diameter of 1½ inch /3.75 cm
- One ½ inch/1.25cm silver metal ring

**Twisted Necklace Cord**— see pages 40-41
- One cord the desired length of the necklace piece, plus 12 inches/30 cm for knotting the ends. The cord shown was made using 4 strands of DMC *Cébélia #10 Crochet Thread* in color #310 Black.

**Needles**
- Tapestry needle size 16
- Chenille needle size 18 or 20

**Finished Measurement:** 1½ inch/3.75 cm drop (not including ring at top)

## BLANDFORD BUTTON PENDANT

### Blandford Button

**Preparation** Thread a tapestry needle with 2 yards/1.8 m of color A thread. Secure the thread to the underside of the ring.

**Step 1—Casting**
Make 120 Cast Knots to cover a 1½ inch/3.75 cm ring.

**Step 2—Slicking**
Gently nudge the knots at the outer edge of the ring to the underside of the ring.

**Step 3—Laying**
Lay 20 equidistant spokes. The ring shown has 20 laid spokes with 4 Cast Knots in between each laid spoke. The spokes will be referred to as spokes 1-20, with spoke 1 in the "12 o'clock" position. Make sure that each spoke has a bottom and a top thread. Secure the thread on the underside of the ring.

**Step 4—Rounding**
Note that the *Dorset Cartwheel* rounds are worked first and then bordered by the *Reverse Cartwheel Wrap* rounds later.

**Rounds 1-2**
Thread a chenille needle with 2 yards/1.8m of color C thread. Secure the thread and work 2 rows of *Dorset Cartwheel Wraps over a Single Spoke* closer to the ring than to the center of the button. Secure and clip the thread.

**Round 3**
Thread a chenille needle with 2 yards/1.8m of color D thread. Commencing at spoke 1, work 1 round of *Reverse Cartwheel Wraps* in a clockwise direction, placing the round between the center of the button and the inner edge of the Dorset Cartwheel rounds.

**Round 4**
Commencing at spoke 1, work 1 round of *Reverse Cartwheel Wraps* in a clockwise direction, placing the second round as close as possible to the ring.

### Pendant Assembly

If necessary, attach a new piece of thread. Switch to the chenille needle, center the metal ring (sideways) and sew it firmly to the top of the button. Secure the thread underneath the ring and clip the thread. Thread the necklace cord through the ring. The necklace shown has a slider knot closure—see page 41.

The **Outer Ring Wrap** button pictured has 84 *Cast Knots*, 12 *Double Laid* spokes, and 24 *Outer Ring Wraps* (12 wraps worked first in a clockwise fashion, then 12 wraps worked in a counterclockwise fashion.)

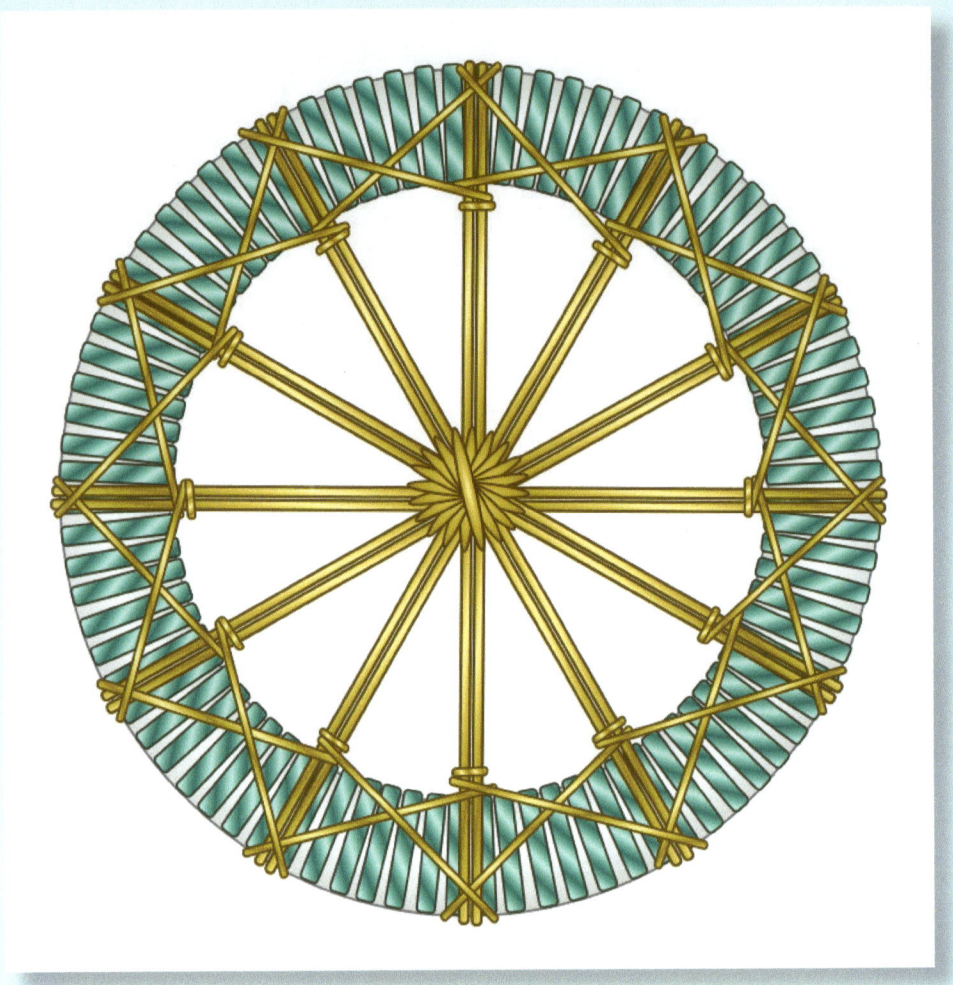

### Outer Ring Wrap —Part 1 Clockwise
(12 spoke ring with spoke 12 in the 12 o'clock position)

**1.** Work close to the ring. Bring the threaded needle up to the front of the button in the space to the left of spoke 12; next, insert the needle down to the back of the ring through the space to the right of spoke 12; finally, bring the threaded needle back up to the front, emerging in the space to the left of spoke 12—first spoke encircled with thread.

**2.** Travel to the next spoke by carrying the threaded needle up and over the ring to the right of spoke 1, and then behind the button. It is helpful to try to nestle this thread in between the spoke and a cast knot on the ring and to keep a finger on it as you continue with this step to hold it in place. Bring the threaded needle up to the front of the button, in the space to the left of spoke 1; next, insert the needle down into the space to the right of spoke 1; finally, bring the threaded needle back up to the front, emerging in the space to the left of spoke 1—second spoke encircled with thread. Repeat step 2 until you have encircled each spoke with thread. End the thread underneath the ring, behind the first spoke that you covered (spoke 12).

# OUTER RING WRAP JEWELRY

**Outer Ring Wrap Part 2 Counterclockwise**
(12 spoke ring with spoke 12 in the 12 o'clock position)
**1.** Work close to the previous round. Bring the threaded needle up to the front of the button, in the space to the right of spoke 12; next, insert the needle down through the space to the left of spoke 12; finally, bring the threaded needle back up to the front, emerging in the space to the right of spoke 12—first spoke encircled with thread.
**2.** Travel to the next spoke by carrying the threaded needle up and over the ring to the left of spoke 11. Bring the threaded needle from behind the button to the front of the button by emerging in the space to the right of spoke 11; next insert the needle down into the space to the left of spoke 12; finally, bring the threaded needle back up to the front, emerging in the space to the right of spoke 12—second spoke encircled with thread. Repeat step 2 until you have encircled each spoke with thread. End the thread underneath the ring, behind the first spoke that you covered (spoke 11).

# PROJECT № 16 OUTER RING WRAP BUTTON EARRINGS

## A DELICATE STAR IS FRAMED BY A SPARKLING TRACERY OF THREAD

### MATERIALS
Each project requires a ruler or tape measure and a small sharp pair of scissors.

**Threads**
- 1 skein DMC *Article #115 Color Variations Pearl Cotton Size 5* in each of color A #4025 Caribbean Bay, and color B #4045 Evergreen Forest
- 1 spool DMC *Diamant* in color C #D3821 Light Gold

**Rings**
- 2 plastic or coated metal rings, each with an outer diameter of 1 inch /2.5 cm

**Jewelry Findings**
- One pair of metal earring hooks in gold

**Needles**
- Tapestry needle size 16
- Chenille needle size 18 or 20

### OUTER RING WRAP BUTTON EARRINGS

**Outer Ring Wrap Button** (Make 2)
**Preparation** Thread the tapestry needle with 2 yards/1.8m of color A thread.

**Step 1—Casting**
Make 72 Cast Knots to cover a 1 inch/ 2.5 cm ring.

**Step 2—Slicking**
Gently nudge the knots at the outer edge of the ring to the underside of the ring. Secure the thread on the underside of the button. Remove the needle. Do not cut the excess thread, as you may wish to use it later.

**Step 3A—Laying**
Thread a chenille needle with a 1 yard/.9m piece of color B thread. Secure the thread to the underside of the ring.

Lay 12 equidistant spokes. The ring shown has 12 laid spokes with 6 Cast Knots in between each laid spoke. The spokes will be referred to as spokes 1-12, with spoke 12 in the "12 o'clock" position. Make sure that each individual spoke has a bottom and a top thread. Secure and clip the thread.

**Step 3B—Anchoring**
Switch colors by threading a chenille needle with a 1 yard/.9m piece of color B thread. Secure the thread to the underside of the center of the button. Anchor and center the spokes in the middle with a few straight stitches. Secure the thread to the back of the button, and clip the thread.

### Outer Ring Wrapping
Thread a tapestry needle with a 2 yard/1.8m piece of color C thread. Secure the thread to back of the ring.

Proceeding in a clockwise direction (from 12 o'clock to 11 o'clock), encircle each spoke with thread using the *Outer Ring Wrapping* technique. When all 12 spokes have been encircled, repeat the *Outer Ring Wrapping* in a counter clockwise direction (from 12 o'clock to 1 o'clock) until all 12 spokes have been encircled with thread.

### Earring Assembly
If necessary, attach a new piece of thread. Switch to the chenille needle, then center the earring hook and sew it firmly to the top of the button. Secure the thread on the underside of the ring and clip the thread.

**Finished Measurement:** 1 inch/2.5 cm drop (not including earring hook)

# PROJECT № 17 OUTER RING WRAP BUTTON WITH CAST RING EARRINGS

## A STELLAR OPTION WITH INCOMPARABLE STYLE AND SOPHISTICATION

**MATERIALS** Each project requires a ruler or tape measure and a small sharp pair of scissors.

### Threads
- 1 skein DMC *Article #115 Color Variations Pearl Cotton Size 5* in color A #4210 Radiant Ruby
- 1 skein DMC *Article #115 Pearl Cotton Size 5* in color B #35 Fuchsia-very dark
- 1 spool DMC *Diamant Grandé* in color C #G3821 Light Gold

### Rings
- 2 plastic or coated metal rings, each with an outer diameter of ½ inch/1.25cm
- 2 plastic or coated metal rings, each with an outer diameter of 1 inch /2.5 cm

### Jewelry Findings
- One pair of metal earring hooks in gold

### Needles
- Tapestry needle size 16
- Chenille needle size 18 or 20

# Outer Ring Wrap and Cast ring Earrings

## Cast rings (Make 2)
**Preparation** Thread the tapestry needle with 1 yard/.9m of color A thread.

**Step 1—Casting**
Make 36 Cast Knots to cover the ring.

**Step 2—Slicking**
Gently nudge the knots at the outer edge of the ring to the underside of the ring.

**Finishing:**
Secure the thread on the underside of the button. Remove the needle. Do not cut the excess thread, as you may wish to use it to attach this ring to another ring. Set ring aside to be used later.

## Outer Ring Wrap Button (Make 2)
**Preparation** Thread the tapestry needle with 2 yards/1.8m of color A thread.

**Step 1—Casting**
Make 72 Cast Knots to cover a 1 inch/2.5 cm ring.

**Step 2—Slicking**
Gently nudge the knots surrounding the outer edge of the ring to the underside of the ring. Secure the thread on the underside of the button. Remove the needle. Do not cut the excess thread, as you may wish to use it to attach this ring to another ring.

**Step 3A—Laying**
Thread a chenille needle with a 1 yard/.9m piece of color B thread. Secure the thread to the underside of the ring.

1. Lay 12 equidistant spokes. The ring shown has 12 laid spokes with 6 Cast Knots in between each laid spoke. The spokes will be referred to as spokes 1-12, with spoke 12 in the "12 o'clock" position. Make sure that each individual spoke has a bottom and a top thread. Secure and clip the thread.

**Step 3B—Anchoring**
Switch colors by threading a chenille needle with a 1 yard/.9m piece of color C thread. Secure the thread to the underside of the center of the button. Anchor and center the spokes in the middle with a few straight stitches (forming a "+" and then an "x", repeating as necessary in a clockwise fashion) Secure and clip the thread.

## Outer Ring Wrapping
**Preparation** Thread a tapestry needle with a 2 yard /1.8m piece of color C thread. Secure the thread to back of ring. Following the instructions for *Outer Ring Wrapping* encircle each spoke in a clockwise, and then counter clockwise direction, until each of the 12 spokes have been encircled. Secure and clip the thread.

## Earring Assembly (Make 2)
**Step 1—Attach the button and Cast ring**
Using the chenille needle, sew one Cast ring to one Dorset button by stitching them together through their adjoining Cast Knots. Secure and clip the threads.

**Step 2—Cover the juncture with thread**
Thread the chenille needle with 1 yard/.9m of color C thread. Attach the thread to the underside of the ring and wrap the juncture (the spot where you attached the button and the ring together) with thread until it is fully covered. Secure and clip the threads.

**Step 3—Attach the earring hook**
Thread the chenille needle with 12 inches /30.5cm of color D thread. Attach the thread to the underside of the ring at the top of the Cast ring, center the earring hook and sew it firmly to the top of the ring. Secure and clip the threads.

**Finishing:**
Secure any loose threads and clip the ends.

**Finished Measurement:** 1½ inch/3.75cm drop (not including earring hook)

# PROJECT № 18 OUTER RING WRAP BUTTON WITH CAST RING BRACELET

## THE PERFECT HINT OF SPARKLE FOR YOUR WRIST

### MATERIALS
Each project requires a ruler or tape measure and a small sharp pair of scissors.

### Threads
- 1 skein DMC *Article #115 Color Variations Pearl Cotton Size 5* in each of color A #4025 Caribbean Bay, and color B #4045 Evergreen Forest
- 1 spool DMC *Diamant* in color C #D168 Light Silver

### Rings
- 2 plastic or coated metal rings, each with an outer diameter of ½ inch/1.25cm
- 2 plastic or coated metal rings, each with an outer diameter of 1 inch/2.5 cm

### Two Part Bracelet Cord — see pages 40-41
- Two cords, each twice the desired length from the Cast ring on the end of the bracelet piece, to the back of the wrist plus 12 inches/30 cm for knotting the ends. The cord shown was made using 4 strands of DMC *Cébélia #10 Crochet Thread* in color #310 Black.

### Needles
- Tapestry needle size 16
- Chenille needle size 18 or 20

# Outer Ring Wrap and Cast Bracelet

## Cast rings (Make 2)
**Preparation** Thread the tapestry needle with 1 yard/.9m of color A thread.

**Step 1—Casting**
Make 36 Cast Knots to cover the ring.

**Step 2—Slicking**
Gently nudge the knots at the outer edge of the ring to the underside of the ring.

**Finishing:**
Secure the thread on the underside of the button. Remove the needle. Do not cut the excess thread, as you may wish to use it to attach this ring to another ring.

## Outer Ring Wrap Button (Make 2)
**Preparation** Thread the tapestry needle with 2 yards/1.8m of color A thread.

**Step 1—Casting**
Make 72 Cast Knots to cover a 1 inch/2.5 cm ring.

**Step 2—Slicking**
Gently nudge the knots surrounding the outer edge of the ring to the underside of the ring. Secure the thread on the underside of the button. Remove the needle. Do not cut the excess thread, as you may wish to use it to attach this ring to another ring.

**Step 3A—Laying**
Thread a chenille needle with a 1 yard/.9m piece of color B thread. Secure the thread to the underside of the ring.

Lay 12 equidistant spokes. The ring shown has 12 laid spokes with 6 Cast Knots in between each laid spoke. The spokes will be referred to as spokes 1-12, with spoke 12 in the "12 o'clock" position. Make sure that each individual spoke has a bottom and a top thread. Secure and clip the thread.

**Step 3B—Anchoring**
Switch colors by threading a chenille needle with a 1 yard/.9m piece of color C thread. Secure the thread to the underside of the center of the button. Anchor and center the spokes in the middle with a few straight stitches (forming a "+" and then an "x", repeating as necessary in a clockwise fashion. Secure and clip the thread.

## Outer Ring Wrapping
**Preparation** Thread a tapestry needle with a 2 yard/1.8m piece of color C thread. Secure the thread to back of ring. Following the instructions for *Outer Ring Wrapping* encircle each spoke in a clockwise, and then counter clockwise direction, until each of the 12 spokes have been encircled. Secure and clip the thread.

## Bracelet Assembly
**Step 1—Sew the button and the two Cast rings together**
Using the chenille needle, sew one Cast ring to each side of the Outer Ring Wrap button by stitching them together through their adjoining Cast Knots. Refer to the picture for placement. Secure and clip the thread.

**Step 2— Cover the junctures with thread**
Thread the chenille needle with 1 yard/.9m of color C thread. Attach the thread to the underside of the ring and wrap the juncture (the spot where you attached the button and the ring together) with thread until it is fully covered. Secure and clip the thread. Repeat for the other juncture.

**Step 3—Attach cord**
Fold one cord in half and make a Lark's head knot to attach it to the Cast ring on the end of the bracelet piece. Make a knot very close to the cut ends of the cord, knotting both ends of the cord together. Repeat with the other cord on the Cast ring on the other end of the bracelet piece. The bracelet shown has a slider knot closure—see page 41.

**Finished Measurement:** 2⅛ inches/5.3 cm across (not including bracelet cord)

# PROJECT № 19 OUTER RING WRAP PENDANT

## THIS COVETABLE PENDANT IS A TRUE SHOW STOPPER

## MATERIALS

Each project requires a ruler or tape measure and a small sharp pair of scissors.

### Threads

***Turquoise and Metallic Gold (pictured on page 85)***

- 1 skein DMC *Article #115 Color Variations Pearl Cotton Size 5* in each of color A #4025 Caribbean Bay, and color C #4045 Evergreen Forest
- 1 spool DMC *Diamant* in color B #D3821 Light Gold

***Burgundy, Pink, and Tangerine***

- 1 skein DMC *Article #115 Pearl Cotton Size 5* in each of color A #3685 Mauve-very dark, color B #603 Cranberry, and color C #742 Tangerine-light

### Ring

- For each: 1 plastic or coated metal ring with an outer diameter of 1½ inch/3.75cm

### Jewelry Findings (for each)

- One ½ in/ 1.25 cm gold metal ring

### Twisted Necklace Cord — see pages 40-41

- One cord the desired length of the necklace piece, plus 12 inches/30 cm for knotting the ends. The cord shown was made using 4 strands of DMC *Cébélia #10 Crochet Thread* in color #310 Black.

### Needles

- Tapestry needle size 16
- Chenille needle size 18 or 20

# Outer Ring Wrap Pendant

## Outer Ring Wrap Button

**Preparation** Thread the tapestry needle with 3 yards/7.5m of color A thread.

**Step 1—Casting**
Make 120 Cast Knots to cover a 1 inch/2.5 cm ring.

**Step 2—Slicking**
Gently nudge the knots at the outer edge of the ring to the underside of the ring. Secure the thread on the underside of the button. Remove the needle. Do not cut the excess thread, as you may wish to use it to attach this ring to another ring.

**Step 3A—Laying**
Thread a chenille needle with a 3 yard/7.5m piece of color B thread. Secure the thread to the underside of the ring.

Lay 12 equidistant triple laid spokes. The ring shown has 12 triple laid spokes with 10 Cast Knots in between each laid spoke. The spokes will be referred to as spokes 1-12, with spoke 12 in the "12 o'clock" position.

Make sure that each individual spoke has 3 bottom and 3 top threads. Secure the thread to the back of the button, and clip the thread.

**Step 3B—Anchoring**
*Burgundy, Pink, and Tangerine Pendant*
Switch colors by threading a chenille needle with a 1 yard/.9m piece of color A thread. Secure the thread to the underside of the center of the button.

*For the Turquoise and Metallic Gold and Burgundy, Pink, and Tangerine Pendant*
Anchor and center the spokes in the middle with a few straight stitches (forming a "+" and then an "x", repeating as necessary in a clockwise fashion) to secure and cover the other threads. It is very important to anchor the spokes as close to the center of the button as possible, or your finished button will not be even. Secure the thread to the back of the button, and clip the thread.

**Step 4—Outer Ring Wrapping**
Thread a tapestry needle with a 3 yard/7.5 m piece of color B thread. Secure the thread to back of the ring.

Working in a clockwise direction (from 12 o'clock to 11 o'clock), encircle each spoke with thread using the *Outer Ring Wrapping* technique.

When all 12 spokes have been encircled, repeat the *Outer Ring Wrapping* in a counter clockwise direction (from 12 o'clock to 1 o'clock) until all 12 spokes have been encircled with thread. Secure and clip the thread

**Step 5—Rounding**
**Rounds 1-3** Working as close to to the ring as possible and commencing at spoke 1, work 1 round of *Single Dorset Cartwheel Wraps* over 1 spoke. Secure and clip the thread

## Pendant Assembly:

If necessary, attach a new piece of thread. Switch to the chenille needle, center the metal ring (facing it sideways, as shown in the picture) and sew it firmly to the top of the button. Secure the thread on the underside of the ring and clip the thread. Thread the necklace cord through the ring. The necklace shown has a slider knot closure—see page 41.

**Finished Measurement:** 1½ inch/3.75cm drop (not including metal ring)

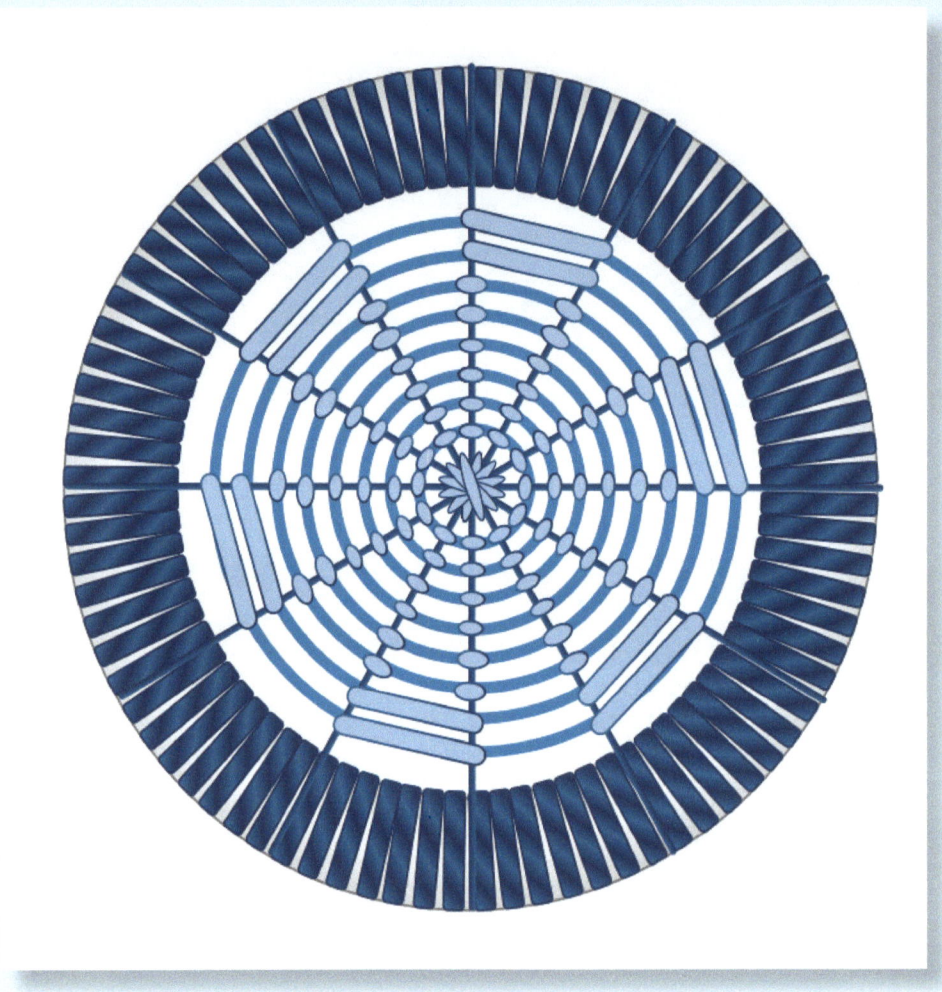

**Single Dorset Cartwheel Wrap Worked Over a Pair of Spokes**
*Working in a clockwise fashion, bring the threaded needle from behind the button through to the space to the right of the first pair of spokes (1-2); next, carry the threaded needle over the top of that pair of spokes and insert the needle into the space to the left of the pair of spokes (1-2); finally slide the threaded needle beneath the pair of spokes that is to the immediate right (3-4) of the pair of spokes (1-2) that was just covered—one *Single Dorset Cartwheel Wrap Worked Over a Pair of Spokes* completed. Repeat from * covering each of the remaining pairs of spokes to complete the round.

# SIX PETAL FLOWER JEWELRY

**The Six Petal Button** pictured to the left has
84 *Cast Knots*, 12 *Laid Spokes*, 6 rounds of *Single Dorset Cartwheel Wrap Worked Over a Single Spoke,* and 2 rounds of *Single Dorset Cartwheel Wrap Worked Over a Pair of Spokes.*

During the *Rounding* step, a *Single Dorset Cartwheel Wrap Worked Over A Pair of Spokes* is made when the working thread goes around (the top and bottom threads) of two spokes at the same time, encircling them completely. For example, a button with 12 spokes would have 6 pairs of spokes, numbered as if on a clock [1-2,3-4,5-6,7-8,9-10,11-12].

# PROJECT № 20 SIX PETAL FLOWER EARRINGS

### FRESH AND FABULOUS ENOUGH THAT YOU WILL WANT A GARDEN FULL OF THESE BOTANICAL WONDERS

## MATERIALS
Each project requires a ruler or a tape measure and a small sharp pair of scissors.

### Threads
- 1 skein DMC *Article #115 Pearl Cotton Size 5* in each of color A #824 Blue-very dark, and color B #827 Blue-very light

### Rings
- 2 plastic or coated metal rings, each with an outer diameter of 1 inch /2.5 cm

### Jewelry Findings
- One pair of metal earring hooks in silver

### Needles
- Tapestry needle size 16
- Chenille needle size 18 or 20

## SIX PETAL FLOWER BUTTON EARRINGS

**Six Petal Flower button** (make 2)
**Preparation** Thread a tapestry needle with 1½ yards/1.4m of color A thread. Secure the thread to the underside of the ring.

**Step 1—Casting**
Make 72 Cast Knots to cover a 1 inch/ 2.5 cm ring.

**Step 2—Slicking**
Gently nudge the knots at the outer edge of the ring to the underside of the ring. Secure the thread on the underside of the button. Remove the needle. Do not cut the excess thread, if you wish to use it to attach this button to the earring hook.

**Step 3A—Laying**
Thread a chenille needle with a 2 yard/1.8 m piece of color B thread. Secure the thread to the underside of the ring.
Lay 12 equidistant spokes. The ring shown has 12 laid spokes with 6 Cast Knots in between each laid spoke. The spokes will be referred to as spokes 1-12, with spoke 12 in the "12 o'clock" position. Make sure that each spoke has a bottom and a top thread.

**Step 3B—Anchoring**
Anchor and center the spokes in the middle with a few straight stitches (forming a "+" and then an "x" repeating as necessary) to secure and align the threads.

**Step 4—Rounding**
Rounds 1-6
Commencing at spoke 1, work 6 rounds of *Single Dorset Cartwheel Wraps* over 1 spoke.

Rounds 7-8
Commencing at spoke 1, work 2 rounds of *Single Dorset Cartwheel Wraps Worked over a Pair of Spokes*. Secure the thread under the button. Remove the needle. Do not cut the excess thread, as you may wish to use it later.

## Earring Assembly
Thread the chenille needle with 12 inches /30.5cm of color A thread. Attach the thread to the underside of the button at the top of the ring, or use the thread ends left from the previous step. Center the earring hook and sew it firmly to the top of the button. Secure and clip all threads.

**Finished Measurement:** 1 inch/2.5 cm drop (not including earring hook)

# PROJECT № 21 SIX PETAL FLOWER BUTTON AND CAST RING BRACELET

## A MASTERFUL COMPOSITION OF A GLIMMER IMBUED BUTTON COMPLEMENTED BY HUED CAST RINGS

### Materials
Each project requires a ruler or tape measure and a small sharp pair of scissors.

### Threads
- 1 skein DMC *Article #115 Pearl Cotton Size 5* in each of color A #828 Blue-ultra very light, and color B #827 Blue-very light
- 1 spool DMC *Diamant Grandé* in color C #G415 Dark Silver

### Rings
- 1 plastic or coated metal ring, with an outer diameter of 1⅛ inches/2.8 cm
- 2 plastic or coated metal rings, each with an outer diameter of ½ inch/1.25 cm

### Twisted Cord Bracelet— see pages 40-41
- 2 pieces of twisted cord cut to desired length plus 12 inches/30.5cm to allow for the knotted ends. The cord shown was made from two pieces of cord each made from 4 strands of DMC *Cébélia #10 Crochet Thread* in color #310 Black.

### Needles
- Tapestry needle size 16 and a Chenille needle size 18 or 20

# Six Petal Flower Button Bracelet

## Cast rings (Make 2)

**Preparation** Thread the tapestry needle with 1 yard/.9m of color B thread.

**Step 1—Casting**
Make 36 Cast Knots to cover the ring.

**Step 2—Slicking**
Gently nudge the knots at the outer edge of the ring to the underside of the ring.

**Finishing**
Secure the thread on the underside of the ring. Remove the needle. Do not cut the excess thread, as you may wish to use it to attach this ring to the button.

## Six Petal Flower Button (Make 1)

**Preparation** Thread a tapestry needle with 1½ yards /1.4m of color A thread. Secure the thread to the underside of the ring.

**Step 1—Casting**
Make 84 Cast Knots to cover the 1⅛ inch /2.8 cm ring.

**Step 2—Slicking**
Gently nudge the knots at the outer edge of the ring to the underside of the ring. Secure the thread underneath the button. Remove the needle. Do not cut the excess thread, as you may wish to use it to attach the button to a Cast ring.

**Step 3A—Laying**
Thread a chenille needle with 2 yards/1.8m piece of color C thread. Secure the thread underneath the ring. Lay 12 equidistant spokes. The ring shown has 12 laid spokes with 7 Cast Knots in between each laid spoke. The spokes will be referred to as spokes 1-12, with spoke 12 in the "12 o'clock" position. Make sure that each spoke has a bottom and a top thread.

**Step 3B—Anchoring**
Anchor and center the spokes in the middle with a few straight stitches (forming a "+" and then an "x", repeating as necessary in a clockwise fashion) to secure and align the other threads. Secure and clip the thread.

**Step 4—Rounding**
Thread a tapestry needle with 1½ yards/1.4m of color B thread. Secure the thread to the underside of the button.

**Rounds 1-6**
Commencing at spoke 1, work 6 rounds of *Single Dorset Cartwheel Wraps* over 1 spoke.

**Rounds 7-8**
Commencing at spoke 1, work 2 rounds of *Single Dorset Cartwheel Wraps Worked over a Pair of Spokes*. Secure the thread on the underside of the ring. Remove the needle. Do not cut the excess thread, as you may wish to use it to attach this ring to the button.

## Bracelet Assembly

**Step 1—Sew the button and the two Cast rings together**
Using the chenille needle, sew one Cast ring to each side of the Six Petal Flower button by stitching them together through their adjoining Cast Knots. Refer to the picture for placement. You may use the excess threads that are already attached to the button and the ring to sew them together, or you may attach a new piece of thread. Secure and clip the thread.

**Step 2—Cover the junctures with thread**
Thread the chenille needle with 1 yard/.9m of color C thread. Attach the thread to the underside of the ring and wrap the juncture (the spot where you attached the button and the ring together) with thread until it is fully covered. Secure and clip the thread. Repeat for the other juncture.

**Step 3—Thread the bracelet cord through the two Cast rings,**
Knot the two pieces of cord together at both ends to make one double cord. Thread the necklace cord through the Cast rings. The bracelet shown has a slider knot closure—see page 41.

**Finished Measurement:** 2⅛ inches/5.3 cm across (not including bracelet cord)

# PROJECT № 22 SIX PETAL FLOWER BUTTON AND CAST RING PENDANT

## THIS SPARKLING PENDANT GLISTENS WITH SILVERY RAYS

## Materials
Each project requires a ruler or tape measure and a small sharp pair of scissors.
### Threads
- 1 skein DMC *Article #115 Pearl Cotton Size 5* in each of color A #33 Fuchsia, and color B #35 Fuchsia-very dark
- 1 spool DMC *Diamant* in color C #D4168 Light Silver

### Rings
- 1 plastic or coated metal ring, with an outer diameter of 1½ inches/3.75cm
- 1 silver plastic or metal ring, with an outer diameter of ½ inch/1.25 cm

### Twisted Necklace Cord — see pages 40-41
- One cord the desired length of the necklace piece, plus 12 inches/30 cm for knotting the ends. The cord shown was made using 4 strands of DMC *Cébélia #10 Crochet Thread* in color #310 Black.

### Needles
- Tapestry needle size 16 and a Chenille needle size 18 or 20

# SIX PETAL FLOWER BUTTON PENDANT

## Cast ring (Make 1)
**Preparation** Thread the tapestry needle with 1 yard/.9m of color B thread.

**Step 1—Casting**
Make 36 Cast Knots to cover the ring.

**Step 2—Slicking**
Gently nudge the knots surrounding the ring to the underside of the ring.

**Finishing**
Secure the thread on the underside of the ring. Remove the needle. Do not cut the excess thread, as you may wish to use it to attach this ring to the button.

## Six Petal Flower Button (make 1)
**Preparation** Thread a tapestry needle with 3 yards /2.7m of color A thread. Secure the thread to the underside of the ring.

**Step 1—Casting**
Make 120 Cast Knots to cover the 1½ inch /3.75 cm ring.

**Step 2—Slicking**
Gently nudge the knots at the outer edge of the ring to the underside of the ring. Secure the thread on the underside of the button. Remove the needle. Do not cut the excess thread, as you may wish to use it to attach the button to a Cast ring.

**Step 3A—Laying**
Thread a chenille needle with a 2 yard/1.8 m piece of color C thread. Secure the thread to the underside of the ring. Lay 12 equidistant spokes. The ring shown has 12 laid spokes with 10 Cast Knots in between each laid spoke. The spokes will be referred to as spokes 1-12, with spoke 12 in the "12 o'clock" position. Make sure that each spoke has a bottom and a top thread.

**Step 3B—Anchoring**
Anchor and center the spokes in the middle with a few straight stitches (forming a "+" and then an "x", repeating as necessary. Secure and clip the thread.

**Step 4—Rounding**
Thread a tapestry needle with 2 yards /1.9m of color B thread. Secure the thread to the underside of the button.

**Rounds 1-8**
Commencing at spoke 1, work 8 rounds of *Single Dorset Cartwheel Wraps* over 1 spoke.

**Rounds 9-11**
Commencing at spoke 1, work 3 rounds of *Single Dorset Cartwheel Wraps Worked over a Pair of Spokes* (see glossary on the previous page). Secure the thread on the underside of the ring. Do not cut the excess thread, as you may wish to use it later.

## Pendant Assembly
**Step 1—Sew the button and the Cast ring together**
Using the chenille needle, sew the Cast ring to the top of the Six Petal Flower button, centering it carefully, and stitching them together through their adjoining Cast Knots. You may use the excess threads that are already attached to the button or you may attach a new piece of thread. Secure and clip all threads.

**Step 2—Cover the juncture with thread**
Thread the chenille needle with 1 yard/.9m of color C thread. Attach the thread to the underside of the ring and wrap the juncture (the spot where you attached the button and the ring together) with thread until it is fully covered. Secure and clip the thread.

**Step 3—Attach the cord**
Make a knot at each end of the cord. Fold the necklace cord in half and make a Lark's head knot to attach it to the Cast ring on the end of the necklace piece. The necklace shown has a slider knot closure—see page 41

**Finished Measurement:** 2 inches/5cm finished pendant length

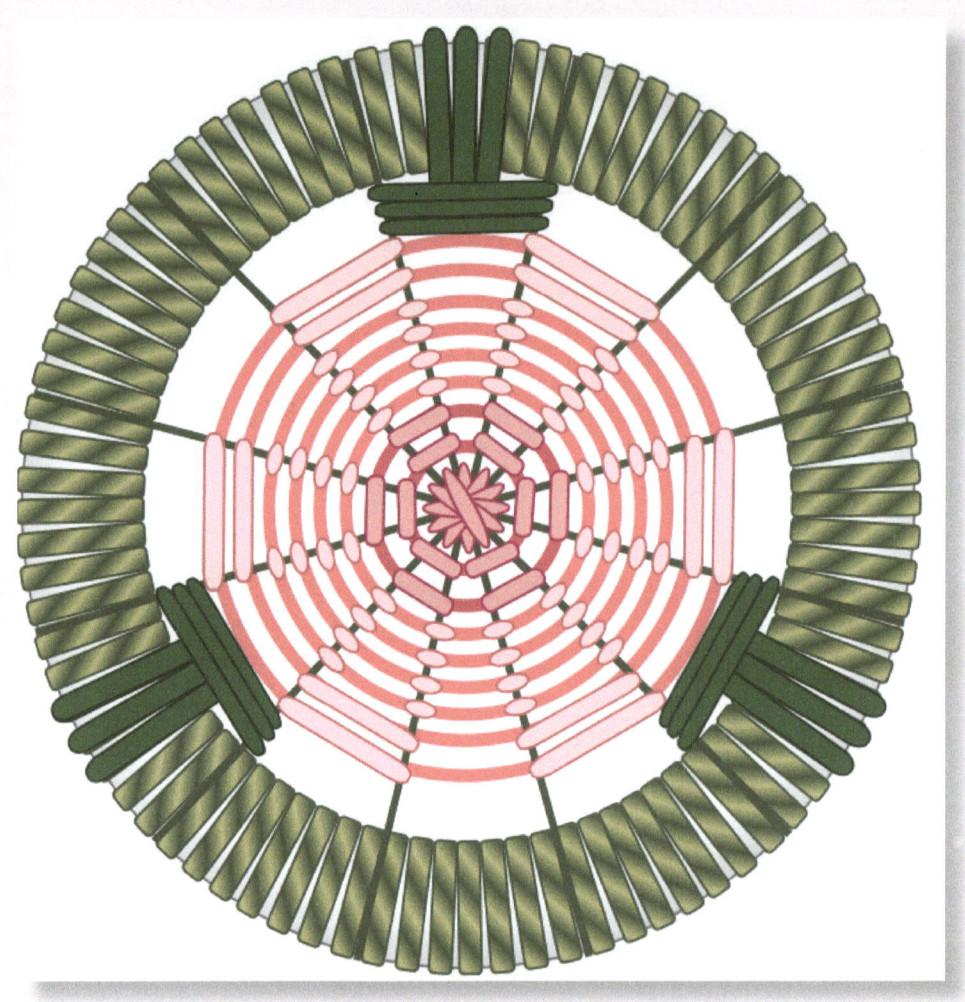

**Flowers and Leaves Button**
with 84 *Cast Knots*, 12 *Laid Spokes*, 2 rounds of *Single Dorset Cartwheel Wrap Worked Over a Pair of Spokes*, 4 rounds of *Single Dorset Cartwheel Wrap Worked Over a Single Spoke*, and 2 rounds of *Single Dorset Cartwheel Wrap Worked Over a Pair of Spokes*.

The leaves are constructed individually: each is wrapped over a pair of spokes, and then over the ring.

# FLOWERS AND LEAVES JEWELRY

**Single Dorset Cartwheel Wrap Worked Over a Pair of Spokes**
*Working in a clockwise fashion, bring the threaded needle from behind the button through to the space to the right of the first pair of spokes (1-2); next, carry the threaded needle over the top of that pair of spokes and insert the needle into the space to the left of the pair of spokes (1-2); finally slide the threaded needle beneath the pair of spokes that is to the immediate right (3-4) of the pair of spokes (1-2) that was just covered—one *Single Dorset Cartwheel Wrap Worked Over a Pair of Spokes* completed. Repeat from * covering each of the remaining pairs of spokes to complete the round.

# PROJECT № 23 FLOWER AND LEAVES BUTTON EARRINGS

## THIS ARTISANAL BLOOM IS AN EVERGREEN DELIGHT

## MATERIALS

Each project requires a ruler or tape measure and a small sharp pair of scissors.

### Threads

*Blue Earrings*

- 1 skein DMC *Article #115 Pearl Cotton Size 5* in each of color A #3012 Khaki Green, color B #826 Blue-dark, color C #827 Blue-very light, and color D #986 Forest Green-very dark

*Lavender Earrings*

- 1 skein DMC *Article #115 Pearl Cotton Size 5* in each of color A #3012 Khaki Green, color B #208 Lavender-very dark, color C #211 Lavender-very light, and color D #986 Forest Green-very dark

### Rings

- 2 plastic or coated metal rings, each with an outer diameter of 1 inch/2.5 cm

### Jewelry Findings (for each)

- One pair of metal earring hooks in silver

### Needles

- Tapestry needle size 16
- Chenille needle size 18 or 20

# Flower and Leaves Button Earrings

**Flower and Leaves Button** (Make 2)
**Preparation** Thread a tapestry needle with 2 yards /1.8 m of color A thread.
**Step 1—Casting**
Make 72 Cast Knots to cover a 1 inch/ 2.5 cm ring.
**Step 2—Slicking**
Gently nudge the knots at the outer edge of the ring to the underside of the ring.
**Step 3A—Laying**
Lay 12 equidistant spokes. The ring shown has 12 laid spokes with 6 Cast Knots in between each laid spoke. The spokes will be referred to as spokes 1-12, with spoke 12 in the "12 o'clock" position. Make sure that each spoke has a bottom and a top thread.
**Step 3B—Anchoring**
1. Anchor and center the spokes in the middle with a couple of straight stitches. Secure and clip the thread.
2. Switch colors by threading a chenille needle with 1 yard/.9m of color B thread. Secure the thread to the underside of the center of the spokes. Anchor and center the spokes in the middle with a number of straight stitches (forming a "+" and then an "x", repeating as necessary in a clockwise fashion) to secure and align the other threads, working until the center is covered with color B thread.
**Step 4A— Rounding**
**Rounds 1-2**
Commencing at spoke 12, work 2 rounds of *Single Dorset Cartwheel Wraps Worked over a Pair of Spokes*.
**Rounds 3-6**
Switch colors by threading a chenille needle with a 2 yard/1.8m piece of color C thread. Secure the thread to the underside of the button. Commencing at spoke 12, work 4 rounds of *Single Dorset Cartwheel Wraps* over 1 spoke.
**Rounds 7-8**
Commence working at spoke 1, work 2 rounds of *Single Wraps Worked over a Pair of Spokes*.
**Step 4B—Rounding the Leaves**
Switch colors by threading a chenille needle with a 1 yard/.9m piece of color D thread. Secure the thread underneath the button.
**Leaf Instructions**
*Bring the threaded needle up to the front of the work to the left of spoke 12 (near round 8.) Wrap the thread four times around this spoke and the spoke to its immediate right, and then wrap the thread three times, completely encircling the ring, right above the leaf wraps—complete leaf made. To travel to the next leaf position, anchor the thread behind the ring, and slide the threaded needle under the work on the back of the button. Repeat from * for leaf 1 (spokes 12-1), leaf 2 (spokes 4-5), and leaf 3 (spokes 8-9). Secure and clip the thread.
**Finishing**
Secure any loose threads and clip the ends.

## Earring Assembly
Thread the chenille needle with a 12 inch/30.5cm piece of color A thread and attach the thread underneath the button at the top of the ring, or use the thread ends left from the previous step. Center the earring hook and sew it firmly to the top of the button. Secure and clip the thread.

**Finished Measurement:** 1 inch/2.5 cm drop (not including earring hook)

# PROJECT № 24 FLOWER AND LEAVES BUTTON WITH CAST RING EARRINGS

### A CAPTIVATING BLOSSOM ADORNS THESE LUXE DROP EARRINGS

## Materials
Each project requires a ruler or tape measure and a small sharp pair of scissors.

### Threads
- 1 skein DMC *Article #115 Color Variations Pearl Cotton Size 5* in each of color A #3012 Khaki Green, color B #3688 Mauve-medium, color C #818 Baby Pink, and color D #986 Forest Green-very dark
- 1 spool DMC *Diamant Grandé* in color E #G3821 Light Gold

### Rings
- 2 plastic or coated metal rings, each with an outer diameter of ½ inch/1.25 cm
- 2 plastic or coated metal rings, each with an outer diameter of 1 inch/2.5 cm

### Jewelry Findings
- One pair of metal earring hooks in gold

### Needles
- Tapestry needle size 16 and a Chenille needle size 18 or 20

**Finished Measurement:** 1½ inch/3.75cm drop (not including earring hook)

# Flower and Leaves Button Earrings

**Cast rings** (Make 2 in color D)
**Preparation** Thread the tapestry needle with 1 yard/.9m of color A thread.
**Step 1—Casting**
Make 36 Cast Knots to cover a ½ inch/1.25cm ring.
**Step 2—Slicking**
Gently nudge the knots at the outer edge of the ring to the underside of the ring.
**Finishing**
Secure the thread underneath the button. Remove the needle. Do not cut the excess thread, as you may wish to use it later.

**Flower and Leaves Button** (Make 2)
**Preparation** Thread a tapestry needle with 2 yards /1.8 m of color A thread.
**Step 1—Casting**
Make 72 Cast Knots to cover a 1 inch/2.5 cm ring.
**Step 2—Slicking**
Gently nudge the knots at the outer edge of the ring to the underside of the ring.
**Step 3A—Laying**
Lay 12 equidistant spokes. The ring shown has 12 laid spokes with 6 Cast Knots in between each laid spoke. The spokes will be referred to as spokes 1-12, with spoke 12 in the "12 o'clock" position. Make sure that each spoke has a bottom and a top thread.
**Step 3B—Anchoring**
1. Anchor and center the spokes in the middle with a couple of straight stitches Secure and clip the thread.
2. Switch colors by threading a chenille needle with 1 yard/.9m of color B thread. Secure the thread to the underside of the center of the spokes. Anchor and center the spokes in the middle with a number of straight stitches (forming a "+" and then an "x", repeating as necessary in a clockwise fashion) working until the center is covered with color B thread.

**Step 4A—Rounding**
**Rounds 1-2** Commencing at spoke 12, work 2 rounds of *Single Dorset Cartwheel Wraps Worked over a Pair of Spokes*.
**Rounds 3-6**
Switch colors by threading a chenille needle with a 2 yard/1.8m piece of color C thread. Secure the thread and commencing at spoke 12, work 4 rounds of *Single Dorset Cartwheel Wraps* over 1 spoke.
**Rounds 7-8**
Commence working at spoke 1, work 2 rounds of *Single Dorset Cartwheel Wraps Worked over a Pair of Spokes*
**Step 4B —Rounding the Leaves**
Switch colors by threading a chenille needle with 1 yard/.9m of color D thread. Secure the thread to the underside of the button.
**Leaf Instructions**
*Bring the threaded needle up to the front of the work to the left of spoke 12 (near round 8.) Wrap the thread four times around this spoke and the spoke to its immediate right, and then wrap the thread three times, completely encircling the ring, right above the leaf wraps — complete leaf made. To travel to the next leaf position, anchor the thread behind the ring, and slide the threaded needle under the work on the back of the button. Repeat from * for leaf 1 (spokes 12-1), leaf 2 (spokes 4-5), and leaf 3 (spokes 8-9). Secure and clip the thread.

**Earring Assembly**
**Step 1—Attach the button and Cast ring**
Using the chenille needle, sew one Cast ring to one Dorset button.
**Step 2—Cover the juncture with thread**
Thread the chenille needle with 1 yard/.9m of color E thread. Attach the thread and wrap the juncture with thread until it is fully covered.
**Step 3—Attach the earring hook**
Thread the chenille needle with 12 inches /30.5cm of color D thread. Attach the thread, center the earring hook and sew it firmly to the top of the ring. Secure and clip the thread.

**Posy Button**
with 84 *Cast Knots*, 12 *Laid Spokes*, 3 rounds of *Single Dorset Cartwheel Wrap Worked Over a Pair of Spokes,* 2 rounds of *Single Dorset Cartwheel Wrap Worked Over a Single Spoke,* and *2* rounds of *Single Dorset Cartwheel Wrap Worked Over a Pair of Spokes, and* 2 rounds of *Single Dorset Cartwheel Wrap Worked Over a Single Spoke.*

# POSY BUTTON JEWELRY

**Single Dorset Cartwheel Wrap Worked Over a Pair of Spokes**
*Working in a clockwise fashion, bring the threaded needle from behind the button through to the space to the right of the first pair of spokes (1-2); next, carry the threaded needle over the top of that pair of spokes and insert the needle into the space to the left of the pair of spokes (1-2); finally slide the threaded needle beneath the pair of spokes that is to the immediate right (3-4) of the pair of spokes (1-2) that was just covered—one *Single Dorset Cartwheel Wrap Worked Over a Pair of Spokes* completed. Repeat from * covering each of the remaining pairs of spokes to complete the round.

# PROJECT № 25 POSY BUTTON EARRINGS

## A CHARMING FLOWER AND FLIRTY FRINGE PROPEL THESE EARRINGS TO FASHION FORWARD

## MATERIALS

Each project requires a ruler or tape measure and a small sharp pair of scissors.

### Threads

*Aqua Earrings*

- 1 skein DMC *Article #115 Color Variations Pearl Cotton Size 5* in color A #4030 Monet's Garden
- 1 spool DMC *Diamant Grandé* in color B #G0415 Dark Silver
- 1 skein DMC *Article #115 Pearl Cotton Size 5* in color C #986 Forest Green -very dark

*Pink Earrings — pictured on page 111*

- 1 skein DMC *Article #115 Color Variations Pearl Cotton Size 5* in color A #4180 Rose Petal
- 1 spool DMC *Diamant Grandé* in color B #G0415 Dark Silver
- 1 skein DMC Pearl Cotton Size 5 in color C #3012 Khaki Green -medium

### Rings

- 2 plastic or coated metal rings, each with an outer diameter of ½ inch/1.25 cm
- 2 plastic or coated metal rings, each with an outer diameter of 1 inch/2.5 cm

### Jewelry Findings (for one pair of earrings)

- One pair of metal earring hooks in silver

### Needles

- Tapestry needle size 16
- Chenille needle size 18 or 20

**Finished Measurements:** 2 inch/5 cm drop (not including earring hook or fringe)
3½ inch/9 cm drop with fringe (not including earring hook)

# Posy Button Earrings

## Cast rings (Make 2 in color A)
**Preparation** Thread the tapestry needle with 1 yard/.9m of color A thread.

**Step 1—Casting**
Make 36 Cast Knots to cover a ½ inch/1.25cm ring.

**Step 2—Slicking**
Gently nudge the knots at the outer edge of the ring to the underside of the ring.

**Finishing:**
Secure, but do not cut the excess thread, as you may wish to use it later.

## Posy button (Make 2)
**Preparation** Thread a tapestry needle with 3 yards/2.7m of color A thread. Secure the thread to the underside of the ring.

**Step 1—Casting**
Make 84 Cast Knots to cover a 1 inch/ 2.5 cm ring.

**Step 2—Slicking**
Gently nudge the knots at the outer edge of the ring to the underside of the ring..

**Step 3A—Laying**
Lay 12 equidistant spokes. The ring shown has 12 laid spokes with 7 Cast Knots in between each laid spoke. The spokes will be referred to as spokes 1-12, with spoke 12 in the "12 o'clock" position. Make sure that each spoke has a bottom and a top thread.

**Step 3B—Anchoring**
1. Anchor and center the spokes in the middle with a few straight stitches (forming a "+" and then an "x"), repeating as necessary. Secure the thread underneath the button. Do not cut the excess thread, as you may wish to use it later.

**Step 4A Rounding**
**Rounds 1-3**
Commencing at spoke 1, work 3 rounds of *Single Dorset Cartwheel Wraps Worked over a Pair of Spokes.*

**Rounds 4-5**
Commencing at spoke 1, work 2 rounds of *Single Dorset Cartwheel Wraps* over 1 spoke.

**Rounds 6-7**
Switch colors by threading a chenille needle with 1 yard/.9m of color B thread. Secure the thread, then skip the first spoke, and commence working at spoke 2, work 2 rounds of *Single Dorset Cartwheel Wraps Worked over a Pair of Spokes.*

**Rounds 8-9**
Switch colors by threading a chenille needle with 1 yard/.9m of color C thread. Secure the thread, and commencing at spoke 1, work 2 rounds of *Single Dorset Cartwheel Wraps* over 1 spoke. Secure and clip the thread.

## Earring Assembly (Make 2)
**Step 1—Sew the button and ring together**
Using the chenille needle, sew one Cast ring to one button by stitching them together through their adjoining Cast Knots. Secure and clip the thread.

**Step 2—Cover the juncture with thread**
Thread the chenille needle with 1 yard/.9m of color B thread. Attach the thread and wrap the juncture (the spot where you attached the button and the ring together) with thread until it is fully covered. Secure and clip the thread.

**Step 3—Attach the earring hook**
Thread the chenille needle with 12 inches /30.5cm of color D thread. Attach the thread under the ring at the top of the Cast ring, center and sew the earring hook to the top of the ring. Secure and clip the thread.

**Step 4—Make the fringe**
Cut 15 6 inch/15cm lengths of color A thread. Stack the cut threads neatly into a bundle. Thread the bundle of threads through the open ring and fold them in half, lining up the ends of the threads evenly.

**Step 5—Cover the juncture with thread**
Thread the chenille needle with 1 yard/.9m of color B thread. Attach the thread and encircle the top of the fringe snugly with 15 wraps. Secure and clip the thread.

# PROJECT № 26  POSY BUTTON BROOCH

### THIS RAVISHING BOUQUET BROOCH IS COMPOSED OF THE MOST RESPLENDENT COLORS

## MATERIALS
Each project requires a ruler or tape measure and a small sharp pair of scissors.
### Threads
- 1 skein DMC *Article #115 Color Variations Pearl Cotton Size 5* in color A #4220 Lavender Fields
- 1 skein DMC *Article #115 Pearl Cotton Size 5* color B #340 Blue Violet-medium, color C #553 Violet, color D #3012 Khaki Green-medium, color E #792 Cornflower Blue-dark,
- 1 spool DMC *Diamant Grandé* in color F #G415 Dark Silver

### Rings
- 1 plastic or coated metal rings, each with an outer diameter of 1½ inch/3.75 cm
- 1 metal ring with an outer diameter of ½ inch/1.25 cm

### Jewelry Findings
- One pin back

### Needles
- Tapestry needle size 16 and a Chenille needle size 18 or 20

**Finished Measurements:** 1½ inch/3.75 cm

# Posy Button Brooch

## Posy button

**Preparation** Thread the tapestry needle with 3½ yards/32m of color A thread.

**Step 1—Casting**

Make 120 Cast Knots to cover a 1½ inch/3.75 cm ring.

**Step 2—Slicking**

Gently nudge the knots at the outer edge of the ring to the underside of the ring. Secure the thread underneath the button. Remove the needle. Do not cut the excess thread, as you may wish to use it later.

**Step 3A—Laying**

Switch colors by threading a chenille needle with 3 yards/2.7m of color B thread. Secure the thread underneath the button. Lay 12 equidistant spokes. The ring shown has 12 laid spokes with 10 Cast Knots in between each laid spoke. The spokes will be referred to as spokes 1-12, with spoke 12 in the "12 o'clock" position. Make sure that each spoke has a bottom and a top thread. Do not clip this thread yet— you will need it for the Rounding step.

**Step 3B—Anchoring**

Switch colors by threading a chenille needle with ½ yard/.45 m of color F thread. Secure the thread underneath the button. Anchor and center the spokes in the middle with a few straight stitches (forming a "+" and then an "x", repeating as necessary in a clockwise fashion). Secure and clip the thread.

**Step 4—Rounding**

**Rounds 1-4**

Using the needle threaded with color A thread from the Laying step and commencing at spoke 1, work 3 rounds of *Single Dorset Cartwheel Wraps Worked over a Pair of Spokes*. Secure and clip the thread.

**Rounds 5-6**

Switch colors by threading a chenille needle with 1 yard/.9 m of color C thread. Secure the thread underneath the button. Commencing at spoke 1, work 2 rounds of *Single Dorset Cartwheel Wraps Worked over a Pair of Spokes*.

**Rounds 6-7**

Commencing at spoke 1, work 2 rounds of *Single Dorset Cartwheel Wraps* worked over a single spoke. Secure and clip the thread.

**Rounds 8-9**

Switch colors by threading a chenille needle with 1 yard/.9 m of color F thread. Secure the thread underneath the button. Skip the first spoke, and commencing at spoke 2, work 2 rounds of *Single Dorset Cartwheel Wraps Worked over a Pair of Spokes*. Secure and clip the thread.

**Rounds 10-12**

Switch colors by threading a chenille needle with 1½ yards/1.3m of color D thread. Secure the thread underneath the button. Starting at spoke 1, work 3 rounds of *Single Dorset Cartwheel Wraps* worked over one spoke.

**Rounds 13-16**

Switch colors by threading a chenille needle with 2 yards/1.8m of color F thread. Secure the thread underneath the button.

1. Commencing at spoke 1, work 2 rounds of *Single Dorset Cartwheel Wraps Worked over a Pair of Spokes*.

2. Skip the first spoke, and commencing at spoke 2, work 2 rounds of *Single Dorset Cartwheel Wraps Worked over a Pair of Spokes*. Secure and clip the thread.

**Rounds 17-20**

Switch colors by threading a chenille needle with 1½ yards /1.3 m of color E thread. Secure the thread underneath the button. Starting at spoke 1, work 3 rounds of *Single Dorset Cartwheel Wraps* worked over one spoke.

## Assemble the Pin

Attach a new thread, or use threads from a previous step. Center the pin back on the underside of the button, and sew it in place. Secure any loose threads and clip the ends.

# GLOSSARY

MANY OF THE TERMS IN THIS BOOK ARE BASED UPON TRADITIONAL NAMES USED IN DORSET BUTTON MAKING. I HAVE ADDED MY OWN LIST OF TERMS IN ORDER TO STANDARDIZE THE PATTERNS IN THIS BOOK.

**ANCHORING:** The step in which the spokes are gathered together in the middle of the button and are held in place by a number of straight stitches that align and center the threads above and beneath the ring.

**CASTING:** The traditional step of covering the ring with knots of thread.

**CAST KNOTS:** The half hitch knots/blanket stitches used during the *Casting* step.

**CLIP:** To cut the secured thread close to the button.

**DOUBLE (OR TRIPLE) LAID SPOKES:** A variation of the *Laying* step when the thread is wrapped two (or three) times around the diameter of the ring to form spokes that will be made up of more than one thread. Wrap the *Double (or Triple) Laid Spoke* spoke so it is placed between two *Cast Knots*, in the same manner as if the spoke was made up of one strand of thread. A *Double (or Triple) Laid Spoke* will be treated as a single spoke for all of the remaining steps in the making of the button. Each *Double Laid Spoke* will have two top threads and two threads underneath the button, and each *Triple Laid Spoke* will have three threads on top of the button and three threads underneath the button.

**JUNCTURE:** The spot where two components (a ring to a ring, a ring to a button, a button to a button) are joined.

**KNOTTING ON A NEEDLE:** Since the blunt tipped tapestry needle is used as both a weight and a grip, and it doesn't have to pierce through anything, it can be helpful to knot the thread to the eye of needle so that the needle does not fall off while you are working. A simple overhand knot works well.

**LARK'S HEAD KNOT:** This is made up of two half hitch knots tied in opposite directions, and is also called a Cow Hitch knot.

**LAYING:** The traditional step of winding thread around the diameter of the ring to form spokes.

**OUTER RING WRAP:** A thread that is wound around the covered ring of a button, for decoration.

**REVERSE CARTWHEEL WRAP:** In this traditional variation of the *Dorset Cartwheel* wrap, the working thread covers two spokes, and is wrapped around one spoke, giving the appearance of the underside of a *Dorset Cartwheel* button *Working in a clockwise direction, bring the threaded needle up from behind the button and emerge to the left of spoke 1; next carry the thread over to the right of the adjacent spoke (spoke 2); finally insert the threaded needle through to the back of the button, and re-emerge to the front of the button up to the left of the spoke just worked. Repeat from * to complete the round.

**ROUND(S):** Refers to a completed circle of the *Rounding* step when working a button.

**ROUNDING:** The traditional step of covering the spokes by wrapping them with thread, one or more at a time.

**SECURING:** The way to attach a new thread at the beginning of a step, or to bury an old thread at the end of a step, so that it will not pull out or unravel. Securing is usually accomplished by means of a few unobtrusive stitches, knots or back stitches underneath the ring or the center of the button.

**SINGLE WRAP(S):** During the *Rounding* step, a single wrap is made when the working thread goes around one spoke, encircling it completely. *Working in a clockwise fashion, bring the threaded needle from behind the button through to the space to the right of the first spoke; next, carry the threaded needle over the top of that spoke and insert the needle into the space to the left of the spoke; finally, slide the threaded needle beneath the spoke to the immediate right of the spoke that was just covered: one single wrap completed. Repeat from * covering each remaining individual spoke to complete the round.

**SINGLE DORSET CARTWHEEL WRAP WORKED OVER A PAIR OF SPOKES:** During the *Rounding* step, a *Single Dorset Cartwheel Wrap Worked Over a Pair of Spokes* is made when the working thread goes around (the top and bottom threads) of two spokes at the same time, encircling them completely. For example, a button with 12 spokes would have 6 pairs of spokes, numbered as if on a clock [1-2,3-4,5-6,7-8,9-10,11-12]. *Working in a clockwise fashion, bring the threaded needle from behind the button through to the space to the right of the first pair of spokes (1-2); next, carry the threaded needle over the top of that pair of spokes and insert the needle into the space to the left of the pair of spokes (1-2; finally, slide the threaded needle beneath the pair of spokes that is to the immediate right (3-4) of the pair of spokes (1-2) that was just covered—one *Single Dorset Cartwheel Wrap Worked Over a Pair of Spokes* completed. Repeat from * covering each of the remaining pairs of spokes to complete the round. This technique may be used on its own or in conjuction with other techniques, such as when creating a *Swanston* button.

**SKIPPING A SPOKE:** This refers to deliberately not working a wrap around a particular spoke, or spokes, bringing the threaded needle under the spoke(s) to get to the next designated spoke before making a wrap.

**SLICKING:** The traditional step in which the bumps of the *Cast Knots* from the *Casting* step are gently nudged behind the ring.

**SPOKE:** A spoke is made up of the corresponding top and bottom threads that emanate from the center point of a ring. Thread spokes are laid across the entire ring (the diameter). Each spoke is made up of a pair consisting of an upper and a lower thread.

A spoke set is made up of two spoke pairs—one spoke pair is named from the center point of the button to the ring in one direction, and a second spoke pair is named from the center point of the button to the ring in the opposite direction.

# INDEX

CONTENTS..................................................................................................................5
THREAD BUTTON JEWELRY.......................................................................................7
HISTORY: From Useful Objects To Unique Embellishments.........................................8
GETTING STARTED — THE MATERIALS....................................................................10
HOW TO CUSTOMIZE YOUR BUTTONS....................................................................13
THE FOUR STEPS OF BUTTON MAKING...................................................................14
Step 1—Casting........................................................................................................18
Step 2—Slicking.......................................................................................................20
Securing the Thread.................................................................................................21
Step 3A—Laying the Spokes....................................................................................22
Step 3B—Anchoring the Laid Spokes......................................................................28
Step 4—Rounding....................................................................................................29
THE VARIATIONS.......................................................................................................31
Variation 1: Single Dorset Cartwheel Wrap Worked Over a Pair of Spokes..............32
Variation 2: Reverse Cartwheel Wrap......................................................................33
Variation 3: Swanston Wrap.....................................................................................35
Variation 4: Outer Ring Wrap...................................................................................37
CONSTRUCTING THE JEWELRY................................................................................39
Cord and Closures....................................................................................................40
THE PATTERNS..........................................................................................................42
DORSET CARTWHEEL JEWELRY................................................................................44
Project # 1  Dorset Cartwheel Earrings...................................................................46
Project # 2  Triple Dangle Earrings..........................................................................48
Project # 3  Dorset Fringe Earrings..........................................................................50
Project # 4  Dorset Cartwheel with Cast Ring Earrings...........................................52
Project # 5  Dorset Cartwheel Brooch.....................................................................56
SWANSTON BUTTON JEWELRY................................................................................58
Project # 6  Swanston Button Earrings....................................................................60
Project # 7  Swanston Button Bracelet....................................................................62
Project # 8  Two Color Swanston Earrings..............................................................64
Project # 9  Cast Ring and Swanston Button Necklace...........................................66
SIMPLE SPOKE JEWELRY..........................................................................................68
Project # 10  Simple Spoke Button Drop Earrings...................................................70
Project # 11  Simple Spoke Pendant........................................................................72

| | |
|---|---|
| BLANDFORD BUTTON JEWELRY | 74 |
| Project # 12  Blandford Button Earrings | 76 |
| Project # 13  Blandford Button Pendant | 78 |
| Project # 14  Blandford Fringe Earrings | 80 |
| Project # 15  Blandford Button Metallic Pendant | 82 |
| OUTER RING WRAP JEWELRY | 84 |
| Project # 16  Outer Ring Wrap Button Earrings | 86 |
| Project # 17  Outer Ring Wrap Button with Cast Ring Earrings | 88 |
| Project # 18  Outer Ring Wrap Button with Cast Ring Bracelet | 90 |
| Project # 19  Outer Ring Wrap Pendant | 92 |
| SIX PETAL FLOWER JEWELRY | 94 |
| Project # 20  Six Petal Flower Earrings | 96 |
| Project # 21  Six Petal Flower Button and Cast Ring Bracelet | 98 |
| Project # 22  Six Petal Flower Button and Cast Ring Pendant | 100 |
| FLOWERS AND LEAVES JEWELRY | 102 |
| Project # 23  Flower and Leaves Button Earrings | 104 |
| Project # 24  Flower and Leaves Button with Cast Ring Earrings | 106 |
| POSY BUTTON JEWELRY | 108 |
| Project # 25  Posy Button Earrings | 110 |
| Project # 26  Posy Button Brooch | 112 |
| GLOSSARY | 114 |

# ACKNOWLEDGEMENTS

I would like to express my most sincere appreciation and gratitude to Tiffany Medina for her invaluable knowledge and gracious assistance with thread selection, Sara Rivers Cofield for permitting me to use the lovely images of the antique British garments from her private collection, exemplary tech editor Janice Meyers, and wonderful models Emily Hassett and Jane Murphy.

## SUPPLIES

All of the needles and threads used in this book are available through the DMC Corporation

www.DMC.com

For updates, information, and button making supplies, please visit:

www.YarnWhirled.com

www.ingramcontent.com/pod-product-compliance
Lightning Source LLC
Chambersburg PA
CBHW040052160426
43192CB00002B/50